T0308672

Documents on
Contemporary Crafts

No. 5

Material Perceptions

Knut Astrup Bull & André Gali (eds.)

NORWEGIAN CRAFTS
2018

Table of Contents

Preface

I am often asked: What is contemporary craft? Sometimes I am asked: What is contemporary craft in relation to fine art, design or folk art? Perhaps the easiest answer is that contemporary craft is art made by artists who focus almost entirely on one type of material, for instance glass, metal, ceramics or textiles. The artists are specialists in their chosen material, and their artistic projects often arise from and are a result of in-depth study of the material itself. The artworks might be connected to everyday life through being functional, or they may reference functionality in some way, or they could be telling stories motivated by political or conceptual ideas.

In Norwegian we have the word *kunsthåndverk,* which directly translates as *art-craft.* I think the Norwegian word is much better than the English term *arts and crafts* because it emphasizes the both-and quality rather than suggesting that art and craft stand in opposition to each other. Internationally, contemporary craft has many names – applied art, material-based art, decorative art, design-led craft and studio craft, to mention a few. What we might define as *contemporary craft* in Norway might be categorized as *design* or *decorative art* or *luxury goods* in other parts of the world. We might not be able to agree on terminology, but more important is that our language be sufficient for communicating about craft and making it accessible. To this end, there is a need for artists, curators and critics working in the field of craft to speak about it, reflect on it, and theorize it in depth, much as we see happening in the field of fine art.

Norwegian Crafts is a vital contributor to the development of craft theory internationally, through producing publications, seminars and online articles. I am proud that we can now present the fifth anthology in the series *Documents on Contemporary Crafts.* The series was initiated by Norwegian Crafts with the aim of producing essay collections on relevant issues within the field of contemporary craft. The first four books have received very good feedback and are being used in educational institutions around the world.

With the present volume's theme of *material perceptions,* the editors have challenged the contributors to share their ideas on how contemporary craft can be perceived in relation to society and everyday life. I would like to thank all the contributors and, in particular, the editors Knut Astrup Bull, senior curator at The National Museum of Art, Architecture and Design in Oslo, and André Gali, head of critical theory and publications at Norwegian Crafts. We are also very grateful to Arts Council Norway for its support, which has enabled us to produce five books in the series *Documents on Contemporary Crafts*.

Hege Henriksen
Director, Norwegian Crafts

Introduction

Over the last two decades, there has been immense development in contemporary crafts, in fact, in the whole field of visual art. On one hand, contemporary crafts have broken free from the constraints of the studio crafts movement and taken new and exciting directions: the art forms range from objects that are closely linked to the tradition of everyday functional objects, to experimental works investigating functional forms, and to conceptual works. In this latter category, a maker may use a variety of media and materials as means for entering into philosophical, social, political, ecological and other discussions.

On the other hand, some contemporary artists have become interested in materials, skills and crafts that are traditionally associated with studio crafts: they engage with material, aesthetical, political and historical aspects stemming from material-based art forms such as ceramics and textile art.

Amongst artists at large, the conceptualization of contemporary crafts and the new interest in craft and materiality have resulted in contemporary crafts increasingly finding a place in an expanded field of art. But are contemporary crafts in this expanded field perceived as crafts or as contemporary art?

Even in the expanded field, contemporary art is characterized by a dualistic mode of perception that clearly marks a division between works of art and everyday objects. The concept of the autonomy of a work of art governs this dualism, and consequently, many works of contemporary craft are excluded from the contemporary field of art. Meanwhile, the more experimental and conceptual works of craft (often with visual similarities to contemporary art) are accepted, even embraced. It is within this context that the question of whether a work is art or craft emerges.

This book contains essays addressing the following questions: Is there a particular way to perceive contemporary crafts that causes them to appear different from contemporary art? When trying to understand and engage with more traditional works of studio craft, has the concept of the autonomous work led to limiting the vocabulary and the field of perception? Are handmade mugs and cups just to be considered nostalgic and antiquated products for the home, or, if we put on a different set of glasses uncoloured by the aforementioned dualism, can they be seen as equally interesting subjects for investigation?

To challenge the concept of the autonomous work when thinking about contemporary crafts, we invited writers who have experience from working with materiality in various contexts to investigate ways of seeing a craft object as a work of non-representational art. Could it be seen as *not* governed by the opposition between art (elevated) and ordinary objects (lowly)? Is it possible to read the craft object in a way that does not disqualify it as art, and if accepting it as art, does not treat it as an autonomous work?

There are a number of commonalities between the contributors to this book. Most notably, they have a tendency to discuss contemporary crafts in relation to aesthetics in a way that alludes to a materialistic tradition. You will find references to philosophers and theorists who are associated with New-materialistic discourses and who challenge the dualism that has marked (and still does) the art discourse and perception of modernity. Another similarity between the authors is that they see craft objects as complex, as simultaneously conceptual and concrete (specific). According to this reading, a craft object is an object for reflection: while neither depicting nor reflecting reality, it enables experiences of realization about our material reality and our bodily sensing of the world.

Throughout the book, you will come across two ways of approaching the questions we address: one begins with seeing crafts as practices, the other with crafts as art forms. Both approaches provide valuable insights into the meaning of materiality within the art institution. Taken as a whole, the book represents *a variety of material perceptions*.

The texts are divided into two groups. Søren Kjørup, Knut Astrup Bull, Sarah R. Gilbert, André Gali and Glenn Adamson enter into epistemological discussions surrounding the perception of contemporary crafts. Anders Ljungberg, Martina Margetts and Hilde Methi discuss art projects that treat materiality as a defining and intended aspect of a work, as well as crucial for the viewer's interpretation of it.

Hilde Methi's text is an exciting contribution to the book in two ways. She discusses an art project which is grounded on New-materialism. The works she describes have a theoretical background that is closely related to that of the other texts in this book, but which also allows the differences between contemporary art and crafts to emerge. Contemporary crafts are generally said to have stronger ties to actual materials, while contemporary art treats such material more abstractly.

The intention of the book is not to argue against including contemporary crafts within the discourses of contemporary art or to present them and discuss them as such. Rather, we want to highlight that contemporary crafts take a materialistic, and not an idealistic, aesthetics as their point of departure. This is why, in our view, contemporary crafts are vital contributions to the expanding field of art, and that the art institution would be one-dimensional, monotonous and poorer without the aesthetic perspectives of contemporary crafts.

Knut Astrup Bull and André Gali
Editors

Art as the Other?
Reflections on Craft's and Fine Art's Places in the Aesthetic Field

Søren Kjørup

The arts – literature, music, painting, sculpture and architecture, traditionally considered the five central ones – constitute an important cultural value in the modern West and in former European colonies. Many of the characteristic norms, styles and institutions of the arts are now also adopted in the increasingly economically and politically important non-Western cultures. The Western book market abounds with translations of non-Western authors' novels, non-Western musicians are educated as virtuosos on Western instruments, and museums of Western-style visual arts are opening everywhere.

This situation seems to support the traditional Western thought that art – or rather Art with a capital 'A' – is an eternal and universal human achievement and cultural value. However, this is an epithet that (if at all) should only be used to describe a more generally conceived aesthetic sensibility and creativity that we meet in many cultural forms and institutional settings at different times and places. One of these – only one amongst many – is what the German-American Renaissance scholar Paul Oskar Kristeller called 'The Modern System of the Arts', more precisely, the way Europeans started to organize and conceive of 'the arts' (or 'fine arts') during the Renaissance, and which did not reach a recognizable form for us today until the mid-eighteenth century.[1]

---

1   See Oskar Kristeller's two-part essay 'The Modern System of the Arts: A Study in the History of Aesthetics', *Journal of the History of Ideas*, vol. 12, no. 4 (1951) and *13* (1) (1952). James I. Porter has lately fiercely attacked Kristeller's essay and thought, claiming that the 'modern' system of the arts is not modern at all, but ancient. See his 'Is Art Modern? Kristeller's "Modern System of the Arts" Reconsidered', *British Journal of Aesthetics*, vol. 49, no. 1 (2009), and the subsequent discussion between Porter and defenders of Kristeller's view, not least Larry Shiner, whose *The Invention of Art: A Cultural History* (Chicago: University of Chicago Press, 2001), has inspired several discussions in this essay, even though it is not explicitly cited.

Kristeller's comprehensive essay focuses on changes in the meaning of the term 'art' and its cognates in Ancient Greek, Latin, Italian, French and so forth, from something like *dexterity* or *skill* (as in 'the art of cooking') up to the modern notion 'that the five "major arts" constitute an area all by themselves, clearly separated by common characteristics from the crafts, the sciences and other human activities',[2] a notion first articulated in 1746 by Charles Batteux in *Les beaux arts réduits à un même principe* ('The fine arts reduced to a single principle'). But Kristeller also sums up the seemingly generally accepted scholarly view (although the popular view about art's eternal position across cultures remains very much alive), that 'such dominating concepts of modern aesthetics as taste and sentiment, genius, originality and creative imagination did not assume their definite modern meaning before the eighteenth century'.[3]

In this article, I consider one special aspect of the modern Western concept of art and the values assigned to it, namely, the relationship between the visual arts and the crafts, after what might be called 'the modern divide' of the aesthetic field between 1500 and 1750. I begin by showing how traditional surveys of 'the history of art' handle the problem that their subject – painting, sculpture and maybe architecture – did not exist as 'fine art' in our sense before the beginning of Modernity. I then develop my main theme, namely that the crafts – ceramics, jewellery and metalworking, glassmaking and works in textile and woodworking – are not only 'the minor arts', 'the lesser arts', 'the applied arts' or 'the decorative arts' (depending on which aspect of these activities is considered) in the modern hierarchical system of the arts, but that they are also seen as what might be called the 'Other' of the fine arts. What this means I shall explain below, and I shall exemplify how the view of craft as the Other shines through in scholarly disciplines like art history and aesthetics.

Immanuel Kant is often cited for asserting that craft is inferior to art. I will argue instead that his main work on aesthetics points elsewhere. But a brilliant spokesperson for modern craft, Glenn Adamson, who is also a contributor to this volume, does indeed take craft's inferiority as a premise for his writing, and this I will show before I reach my

---

2   Charles Batteux, *Les beaux arts réduits à un même principe*
     (Durand: Paris, 1746).

3   Kristeller, 'The Modern System', 496–497.

concerning consideration: Would it give a more faithful picture of the places of craft and fine art in the aesthetic field if we turned the hierarchy upside down, such that the fine arts were seen as the Other of craft?

Art before Art – and later

If visual 'art' in our modern European sense has only existed since the mid-eighteenth century, one should expect historical surveys of visual art written for a modern European readership to begin around 250 years ago, maybe with a view back to forerunners since the Renaissance. However, few surveys claiming to be histories of art – the very first one being J.J. Winckelmann's *Geschichte der Kunst des Altertums* ('History of Ancient Art') from 1764 [4] – limit themselves in that way.

The dilemma of visual arts historians who want their surveys to start before the birth of the modern concept should be evident: one may do what Winckelmann did, namely, concentrate on works that, although ancient, seem to fit into the modern concept of art (in Winckelmann's case nearly only sculpture), but obviously this is an ahistorical approach that will cause a modern audience to misunderstand the pre-modern aesthetic field. Alternatively, one could write a 'history of art' that presents the pre-modern aesthetic field on its own premises, but just as obviously, this would not be writing a history of art in the modern sense of 'art' that the audience takes for granted.

The common solution to the dilemma is something in-between: the closer we get to the Renaissance, the more the author of a survey of the history of art is likely to concentrate on painting and sculpture (perhaps also architecture), and the further back the survey starts, the broader the scope of objects that are mentioned and discussed. As we approach the late Middle Ages and the Renaissance, the scope will slowly and silently be narrowed. However, that the concept of art – the alleged subject of the histories – slowly changes as the story develops is rarely made explicit.

---

4   J.J. Winckelmann, *Geschichte der Kunst des Altertums* (Walther: Dresden, 1764).

Please browse through some popular surveys of the history of art.[5] Typically, they start 25,000 years ago with an 11-cm-high figurine, the so-called *Venus from Willendorf*, or at least with the 15,000-year-old cave paintings of Southern France and Northern Spain. Many such histories, especially if they call themselves histories of 'world art', have oblique early glances to Pre-Columbian American 'art' or to African 'art' (the latter often surprisingly recent works like nineteenth-century masks), maybe even to Maori tattooing, with much guesswork about these works' religious and ritualistic meanings and uses. Then they concentrate on the grand European narrative, starting with ancient Egypt and the well-known route through ceramics, metalwork, textile, sculpture and paintings from Greek and Etruscan, Roman and Medieval 'art', up to the Western Renaissance and usually a work like the famous elaborate salt cellar that Benvenuto Cellini created around 1540 for the French king François I. But after the salt cellar, the rich repertoire of artefacts suddenly disappears. We are left mostly with painting and sculpture (plus a few drawings and prints and even fewer examples of interior decoration, namely art galleries).

And not only do all kinds of craft products disappear; all other aspects of the included paintings and sculptures than those directly connected to them as aesthetic objects seem to vanish precisely when we might have moved from guesswork to empirical knowledge. We get sketches of the artists' biographies, reflections on style and technique, iconographic interpretations and a few remarks on the art market, but very little that could replace the mostly religious interpretations of 'works of art' from the Stone Age, for instance, about how all these post-Renaissance works played a role in their owners' daily lives or in society at large.

Craft as the Other
But craft did not vanish from Earth just because it vanished from art historical surveys the moment they stepped into Modernity. Western craftspersons did not stop making vessels, tombstones, coins,

---

5   Three examples are E.H. Gombrich, *The Story of Art* (London: Phaidon, 1950); Hugh Honour and John Fleming, *A World History of Art* (London: Macmillan, 1982); and H.W. Janson, *History of Art: A Survey of the Major Visual Arts from the Dawn of History to the Present Day*, revised and enlarged edition (London: Thames and Hudson, 1969).

clothing, furniture, tapestries, utensils, book covers, jewellery, candle sticks, salt cellars and all those other things they had been credited with before, not even when production of some such artefacts moved from individuals and cottages to organized, divided labour in factories like the ones for porcelain in Meißen and Sèvres. And people did not stop tattooing one another, if that remained their cultural obligation, once the art historical surveys reached the Renaissance and Enlightenment.

Obviously, craft continued to exist as the other side of the modern divide within the aesthetic field, mostly in its own departments or institutions, next to those of fine arts. Once the fine arts were firmly established with their academies, salons and museums during the seventeenth and eighteenth centuries, the crafts followed suit in the nineteenth century with their 'arts and crafts' schools, fairs and museums. But now and then craft also turns up as a double, a shadow or a menace, even within the institution of fine art itself. It sneaks into artistic practice, into artistic theory and into critical writing about the fine arts.

It is an old and quite fundamental – although rather banal – thought in logic and philosophy that something is defined not only through what it is, but also equally through what it is not. At least during the last two hundred years, however, it has been pointed out that the initially rather neutral positioning of one thing towards the other, the differing one, may take on an aspect of hierarchy, and that the hierarchy may even be turned on its head or display a weird dialectic.

G.W.F. Hegel discussed this dialectic in a passage on the master and his slave (in §§ 190–191 in his *Phänomenologie des Geistes*, 'Phenomenology of Mind', 1807).[6] The master, said Hegel, is only the master if he is recognised as such by his slave. In an uncanny sense, therefore, the slave has the upper hand in this relationship. But we also know fairy tales of situations where the hierarchy is not completely turned upside down, but where the Other appears as a menacing figure, a doppelgänger, a shadow or a temptation that threatens the identity of the main character, a heinous Mr. Hyde to the decent Dr. Jekyll.

---

6   G.W.F. Hegel, *Phänomenologie des Geistes* (1807), vol. 3 of *Werke*
    (Frankfurt am Main: Suhrkamp, 1970), 145–155.

We meet this conception of craft as the Other of the fine arts in many very different disguises – or not disguised at all, but clearly spelled out, as when professors and their students of fine art in old-fashioned art academies protest fiercely against plans of merging their noble institution with a less noble school of arts and crafts. Nearly always, when somebody utters his or her fear of the fine arts becoming 'impure', it is when artists put what some feel as too much energy into one of the three main characteristics of what we normally would call craft in the modern world: *skill*, the *decorative* and the *functional*.

The Other in art history and in the philosophy of art

Let us now consider two examples of what the contempt or fear of what craftspeople see as the values of their profession looks like in early traditional art history and in the modern philosophy of art. One of the first professional German art historians (in the generation just after that of the founders of the German academic history of art: Karl Schnaase, Franz Theodor Kugler and Gustav Friedrich Waagen) was Wilhelm Lübke, who published the first edition of his *Grundriß der Kunstgeschichte* in 1860 (English translation *Outlines of the History of Art*, 1878).[7] Like many art historians after him, Lübke writes about Benvenuto Cellini, and not only about his salt cellar, but also about his sculptures, for instance, his life-size statues in silver and his colossal *Mars*. None of these have survived to 'our time', we read, but they 'probably did not rise over a common *decorative* level'[8] – obviously, they were to be considered as overgrown figurines rather than as genuine works of fine art. And about Cellini's *Perseus with the Head of Medusa* in the Loggia dei Lanzi in Florence, he writes that 'although in its meticulous treatment [it is] not without naturalistic awkwardness, yet with a happy line and a powerful expression'.[9] Fortunately, Cellini's rather clumsy insistence on demonstrating a craft competence such as skill has not weakened the aesthetic value of the work as fine art, it seems.

---

7   Wilhelm Lübcke, *Grundriß der Kunstgeschichte* (1860),
    2nd ed. (Stuttgart: Ebner & Seubert, 1864).
8   Ibid., 535 (my translation and italics).
9   Ibid.

In the philosophy of art, the clearest example of casting craft in the role of the Other of art can be found in the English philosopher R.G. Collingwood's *The Principles of Art* from 1938.[10] Collingwood even discusses theories of craft as the Other of aesthetic theory. His book is written with an explicit purpose:

> (...) to clear up our minds as to the distinction between art proper, which is what aesthetic is about, and certain other things which are different from it but are often called by the same name. Many false aesthetic theories are fairly accurate accounts of these other things, and much bad artistic practice comes from confusing them with art proper. These errors in theory and practice should disappear when the distinctions in question are properly apprehended.

In the book's first part, Collingwood tries to clear the ground, and the first chapter (Chapter II, because the introduction to the book is called Chapter I) is used to disentangle 'Art and Craft'. He begins by enumerating what he sees as the main characteristics of craft, the leading theme being that '[c]raft always involves a distinction between means and end' and 'between planning and execution',[11] and that the craftsperson always works with a purpose in mind, turning 'raw material' into artefacts by giving form to matter.[12] Understanding art as craft is to subscribe to the false 'Technical Theory of Art', known from antiquity (Plato, Aristotle and Horace), but certainly also noticed by Collingswood in his own time:

> Present-day fashions of thought have in some ways even tended to reinforce it. We are apt nowadays to think about most problems, including those of art, in terms either of economics or of psychology; and both ways of thinking tend to subsume the philosophy of art under the philosophy of craft.[13]

Collingwood's rather narrow concept of what he calls 'craft' is then amplified in the next three chapters where he disentangles art proper

---

10 R.G. Collingwood, *The Principles of Art*
    (London: Oxford University Press, 1963 [1938]).

11 Ibid., 15.

12 Ibid., 16.

13 Ibid., 19.

from mere 'literal' representations (a question of skill, simply),[14] from what he calls 'magic' (any form of 'quasi-artistic' means for arousing 'useful' emotions),[15] and from amusement (arousing joyful emotions that have a value in themselves).[16] One might say that these other forms (and misunderstandings of 'art proper', Collingwood would say) are also forms of craft, and Collingwood actually writes about 'magic', asserting that 'artistic activities like dances, songs, drawing or modelling' belong to magic (as they belong to amusement), so they 'are means to a preconceived end, and are therefore not art proper but craft'.[17]

But what is art proper to Collingwood? What is a genuine artistic activity? It is, he says, 'the experience of expressing one's emotions'.[18] This is a very narrow concept indeed, and one that may be attacked from many angles – but that is not the point here. The point is that Collingwood somehow sees craft with its purposes as a disturbing factor everywhere around him when he is on the lookout for 'art proper'.

Kant against craft?

That art should be without any purpose, and that this perspective is one aspect of a principled difference between craft and the fine arts, is a thought often attributed to the German Enlightenment philosopher Immanuel Kant by theoreticians in this field. Many seem to remember that in his *Kritik der Urteilskraft* (1790, in English *Critique of Judgment*),[19] he put forward a series of criteria for works of art that make a clear distinction between these works and other products of human ingenuity. Did he not demand that real works of fine art should not generate any kind of interest or have any purpose, and in that sense, should be 'pure'? And obviously, products of craft are things we are interested in, not least because we need them for their intended purpose. Consequently, however much artistry and skilfulness have been invested in them, they remain 'impure'.

---

14 Ibid., 43–46.

15 Ibid., 65–66.

16 Ibid., 78.

17 Ibid., 65.

18 Ibid., 275.

19 Immanuel Kant, *Kritik der Urteilskraft*, *Werke*, vol. 2
(Darmstadt: Wissenschaftliche Buchgesellschaft, 1966 [1790]).
I quote the English translation by J.H. Bernard, *The Critique of Judgment*, 2nd ed. (London: Macmillan, 1914).

The Swedish contemporary artist and theoretician Lars Vilks is one of many commentators who have used Kant to highlight the difference between art and craft. In the essay 'Mellom kunst og håndverk' ('Between Art and Craft') from 1999 (published in *Kunsthåndverk*, the magazine of the Norwegian Association for Arts and Crafts), Vilks partly claims, partly reports Kant as claiming as much:

> The arts and crafts only exist as 'lower' forms of art, applied art in different forms. Fundamentally, applied art is a hybrid of craft and art. It has a certain utility and at the same time has to exist as an aesthetic object. In other words, it becomes impure.[20]

Vilks, however, like many others with fuzzy recollections of Kant's aesthetics, seems to have forgotten that Kant's *Critique of Judgment* is not about art (and its rivals) at all, but – as the title suggests – about making judgments, in this case judgments about purposive phenomena, in culture and in nature. It has two parts. The second (about a third of the text, and read by only a very few specialists today) is about phenomena in nature that have a purpose in themselves, for instance, living beings, who (we might say colloquially) just live to be alive. The first, cultural, part is the aesthetic one; however, it is not concerned with *art*, but with *taste*. What Kant here discusses is how we 'judge' two different aesthetic qualities: beauty, which pleases in a special, reflective way, and the sublime, which makes us shiver in an especially delightful (yet frightened) way.

To show just how far Kant is from discussing works of art, let me quote a passage of examples of what he is thinking of. These examples also show that what should have no purpose and be constrained by no concept is the 'free beauty', not the work of art:

> Flowers are free natural beauties. Hardly anyone but a botanist knows what sort of a thing a flower ought to be; and even he, though recognising in the flower the reproductive organ of the plant, pays no regard to this natural purpose if he is passing judgement on the flower by Taste. There is then at the basis of this judgement no perfection of any kind, no internal purposiveness, to which the collection of the manifold is referred. Many birds (such as the parrot, the humming bird, the bird of paradise), and many sea shells

20 Lars Vilks, 'Mellom kunst og håndverk',
   Kunsthåndverk, no. 1 (1999), 27 (my own translation).

are beauties in themselves, which do not belong to any object determined in respect of its purpose by concepts, but please freely and in themselves. So also delineations á la grecque, foliage for borders or wall-papers, mean nothing in themselves; they represent nothing – no Object under a definite concept, – and are free beauties.[21]

Kant also gives examples of the focus for the sublime judgment:

[b]old, overhanging, and as it were threatening, rocks; clouds piled up in the sky, moving with lightning flashes and thunder peals; volcanoes in all their violence of destruction; hurricanes with their track of devastation; the boundless ocean in a state of tumult; the lofty waterfall of a mighty river, and such like.[22]

Admittedly, towards the end of the aesthetic part of the *Critique of Judgment*, we do find some sections on 'art', for instance § 43, and two pages 'Of art in general'. These pages turn out not to be about paintings, poems and preludes, however, but about all kinds of productive activities that demand special knowledge and other competencies, in short, they are about art in the ancient sense.[23] And what is important here is that Kant consistently writes about art as *activities*, not as *results* of activities. This is also the case when Kant uses a few pages to discuss what is meant by 'beautiful art'.[24] He writes for instance about 'the purposiveness in the product of beautiful art'.[25]

The only treatment of what we would call 'the fine arts' in Kant's *Critique of Judgment* is found in three paragraphs towards the end of the aesthetic part, § 51 'Of the division of the beautiful arts',[26] § 52 'Of the

---

21 Kant, *Critique of Judgment*, 81 (§ 16, italics in the original).

22 Ibid., 125 (§ 28).

23 In the English translation, Kant makes a distinction between 'art' and 'handicraft' (p. 184), a distinction that may fool the careless reader into thinking that he makes a distinction between art and craft. The German original, however, has 'Kunst' and 'Handwerk' here (p. 156), and in his comments concerning the distinction, Kant discusses whether watchmaking should be categorized as art and smithing as craft. It is then obvious that we are still far from the modern distinction within that aesthetic field.

24 Kant, *Critique of Judgment*, 185–190 (§§ 44–46).

25 Ibid., 188. But even today we talk of artworks as 'works of art' where, to make literal sense of the expression, 'art' must mean an activity.

26 Ibid., 206–213.

combination of beautiful arts in one and the same product'[27] (songs combining text and music, etc.) and § 53 'Comparison of the respective aesthetical worth of the beautiful arts'.[28] Here are well-known opinions and themes that clearly point backwards in history (for instance to the competition between the various art forms in § 53, a pastime – the *paragone* – known at least from the Renaissance in writings by Alberti, Dürer and Leonardo). But there are also surprises for the theoretician who expects Kant to condemn craft and to elevate fine art, not least in the examples he gives of what he sees as belonging to the various forms of art.

In most histories and theories of the visual arts,[29] architecture is discussed in connection with sculpture and painting, and we find the same in Kant, even though he does have a small reservation because of the purposefulness of the building activity. However, noteworthy is that his concept of the art of architecture makes a big stride into the field that we tend to leave to craft:

> Temples, splendid buildings for public assemblies, even dwelling-houses, triumphal arches, columns, mausoleums, and the like, erected in honourable remembrance, belong to Architecture. Indeed all house furniture (upholsterer's work and such like things which are for use) may be reckoned under this art; because the suitability of a product for a certain use is the essential thing in an *architectural work*.[30]

In other words, while the traditional history of art stops at the buildings, Kant also integrates all kinds of crafted objects that make the building useable, into his concept of 'beautiful art'. And he does so, obviously, not to put all this 'house furniture' into a lower category, but on the contrary, to see it as part of the arts.

We get the same kind of surprise regarding painting. The category of painting must be divided into two subcategories, Kant argues, namely 'painting proper' and – landscape gardening! In a long footnote, Kant admits that gardening may seem a strange sub-category of painting, but both here and in the main text, he explains what he

27 Ibid., 214–215.
28 Ibid., 215–220.
29 Kant writes about 'die bildende Künste', which J.H. Bernard translates into 'the formative arts'.
30 Kant, *Critique of Judgment*, 210 (italics in the original).

thinks about 'ornamentation of the soil with a variety of those things (grasses, flowers, shrubs, trees, even ponds, hillocks and dells)' that are 'only apparent to the eye, like painting'.[31] And he even adds:

> Under painting in the wide sense I would reckon the decoration of rooms by the aid of tapestry, bric-a-brac, and all beautiful furniture which is merely available to be *looked* at; and the same may be said of the art of tasteful dressing (with rings, snuff-boxes, etc.). For a bed of various flowers, a room filled with various ornaments (including under this head even ladies' finery), make at a fete a kind of picture; which, like pictures properly so-called (that are not intended to *teach* either history or natural science), has in view merely the entertainment of the Imagination in free play with Ideas, and the occupation of the aesthetical Judgment without any definite purpose.[32]

In this passage, I especially like how Kant expands the daily-life aesthetics all the way through accessories and fashion.

'Art is not craft'
One tempting conclusion here would be that we should stop making a principled distinction between art and craft and just include the various crafts within the already motley repertoire of art forms, genres, sub-genres and 'minor' genres. Yet so far, crafts that involve materials like metal, clay, glass or textile are not generally accepted as arts, although certain works by recognized artists like Gauguin or Picasso may appear in contemporary art museums, in survey histories of contemporary art and in journals focussing on the contemporary fine arts. But specialized textile artists, ceramicists, jewellers, etc. – no way![33]

Nevertheless, even the most artistically ambitious contemporary craftspersons do not seem keen to acquire the denomination 'artist' or to have their work discussed as 'fine art', but instead prefer to be named according to the material they use (or in which they have their

---

31 Ibid., 211.

32 Ibid.

33 In art museums, exhibitions of works by prominent fashion designers are not completely unknown from recent years when museum directors want to draw new groups of audiences to their institutions. An example could be the exhibition of works by the Paris-based Norwegian Per Spook in the Museet for Samtidskunst ('Museum for Contemporary Art') in Oslo in 2006. However, a permanent exhibition of 20 dresses by Spook is now in the costume galleries of the Norwegian Museum of Decorative Arts and Design.

background, education, etc.): textile artist, ceramicist, jeweller, etc.[34] And the same position is taken by one of the most perceptive contemporary theoreticians of craft that I know of, the already mentioned Glenn Adamson.

Adamson bases his discussion of craft in his book *Thinking Through Craft* (2007)[35] on the obvious marginal position of craft (the way I have done above, but he uses slightly different concepts). Naively, one might have expected a high-profile craft author and curator like Adamson to argue for a position of craft – and at least modern studio craft – amongst the arts, but no: the value of craft within the contemporary aesthetic field is precisely in its position as a kind of horizon only, 'a conceptual limit active throughout modern artistic practice'.[36] And the question of whether craft is art is spurious:

> Anything can be taken for art, craft included, and that is all there is to say on the matter. But as surely as this is a banal truism, the opposite proposition, that art is *not* craft – that it might gain something by defining itself against that category, is a rather interesting one.[37]

Based on this position, Adamson writes about craft from five well-known but quite imaginatively developed perspectives. 'First, while the modern artwork has usually been held to be autonomous, the work of craft is *supplemental*'[38] – theoretically his most important point – is obviously inspired by the French philosopher Jacques Derrida, and I shall return to this 'supplementarity of craft' below. Second, where artistic practice has normally been oriented towards optical effects, craft is organized around *material* experience.[39] The third angle is *skill*, an indispensable concept in connection with craft. And finally,

---

34 This goes at least for Caroline Slotte and Kjell Rylander, two
  ceramicists who were members of the 2009–11 research group K-verdi
  ('Art value: A research project on trash and readymades, art and ceramics',
  see https://www.facebook.com/K-verdi-140852149322667/, accessed
  16 January 2018) and for all other craftspeople that I have met while
  I was a member of the group.
35 Glenn Adamson, *Thinking Through Craft* (London: Berg, 2007).
36 Ibid., 2.
37 Ibid. (italics in the original).
38 Ibid., 4 (italics in the original).
39 Ibid.

Adamson writes about the *pastoral* side of craft, dating back to the Arts and Crafts Movement of the late nineteenth century, and still alive, and of the different theoretical roles of *amateurism* (including *feminism*) in craft and in art.[40]

Adamson reaches his point about the Derridarian supplementarity of craft by way of the German dialectical philosopher and cultural critic Theodor Adorno. Adorno is primarily known as a promoter of the most elitist and 'incomprehensible' avant-garde art (which he saw as a necessary protest against modern capitalist consumer culture), but Adamson points out that he also found it necessary to have 'a precise understanding of the materials and techniques at the artist's disposal'.[41] In Adamson's words, Adorno argued that 'craft must be a self-abnegating path to the creation of something beyond itself'.[42] Against Adamson, however, one may wonder whether Adorno was concerned with craft at all as a creative activity that produces valuable aesthetic works in their own right, or whether he was rather discussing the skill necessary to produce valuable art.

As Adamson reads him, Adorno claims that craft is distinct from art but nevertheless a 'supplement' to the artwork (in Derrida's sense of 'supplement' as first proposed in his early *De la grammatologie*).[43] Adamson's definition runs thus: 'A supplement is that which provides something necessary to another, "original" entity, but which is nonetheless considered to be extraneous to that original.' [44] The supplementarity is thus related to my concept of craft as the Other of art in the sense that craft (from the viewpoint of art, I would add) is both extraneous and bound to the artwork, but the difference between the concepts is that as supplement, craft is not threatening, but rather is a welcome necessity for art. Strangely, although the title of his book suggests a craft perspective, Adamson does not consider how art looks from the viewpoint of craft.

At any rate, what Adamson hopes is 'to redirect the debate about craft by focusing on its subordination'.[45] He continues:

---

40 Ibid.

41 Ibid., 10.

42 Ibid., 11.

43 Jacques Derrida, *De la grammatologie* (Paris: Minuit, 1967).

44 Adamson, *Thinking through Craft*, 11.

45 Ibid., 4.

Understandably, partisans of the crafts are unlikely to see craft's second-class status within art theory as something to accept at face value, but this resistance has also led to a lack of serious thought about craft's inferiority relative to art. While art is a matter of nomination within an infinite field – that is, art is anything that is called art – craft involves self-imposed limits. Modern art is staked on the principle of freedom, its potential transcendence of all limits, including (even especially) those of craft. Yet in the very marginality that results from craft's bounded character, craft finds its indispensability to the project of modern art. My central argument, when all is said and done, is that *craft's inferiority might be the most productive thing about it*.[46]

However tempting it is to take this very Hegelian position – the slave's power comes from his inferiority – I think there is a more radical way of turning the traditional hierarchy of craft and art on its head, a more oppositional picture that can be given of the history of the (first of all) European (and more and more generally Western) aesthetic field since the Middle Ages. That is what I shall suggest in the next and last section of this essay.

Art as the Other?

Here is the traditional story: During the period 1500–1750, the old European cohesive aesthetic field of visuality is divided into the fine arts and the crafts, respectively, two separate aesthetic realms. This essay's main point thus far has been that craft has not only been considered as the lower level of the modern aesthetic hierarchy with fine art on top, but also as the annoying Other of Art (while Glenn Adamson would say the necessary supplement of art). But maybe there is something fundamentally wrong with the traditional story, yet not in the old-fashioned, anti-Kristeller sense that the concept of fine art is universal and dates back to time immemorial, but for instance, in the sense that the hierarchy is not what it seems to be.

Just a few observations may suggest that there is something wrong with the traditional story, empirically, theoretically and in the connection between what we see and what we say, all of it suggesting that the great divide between fine art and craft has never been completely accomplished.

---

46 Ibid. (italics in the original).

It is indeed the case that institutionally, the fine arts academies, dating to the sixteenth century, are quite separate from the craft schools that did not arise until the nineteenth century, more or less in reaction to the Industrial Revolution. However, it is also the case that traditional fine arts academies let the creativity of their students loose only after years of training in basic craft-like skills, not only in copying and drawing from models and from life, constructing perspective and the like, but also in handling canvasses, paint, stone, metals and so forth.

It is also the case that major artists like Michelangelo or Rubens might rise to the highest ranks of society – or at least might be socially connected to these ranks. Yet their work was not confined to fine art (in the strict sense) like painting or sculpture, but included things such as interior decoration and arranging spectacular events, things we would consider as crossing the line into craft. And the elevated position of these and other artists was indeed exceptional, for most painters and sculptors have been confined to small formats, small incomes and modest positions in rather local surroundings – just like artisans have been.

Finally, the modern system of the arts is not at all as clear-cut as the history and philosophy of art might suggest. We have the question of which genres belong even amongst the visual arts: Batteux included only painting and sculpture (not architecture) among the fine arts. But what about drawings, prints and photographs? What about statuettes and figurines? Does size play a role regarding the basic categorization? And we have the question of quality: 'Painting' is said to belong amongst the fine arts, but does that mean any kind of coloured canvas? It is easy to mention single examples of craft products that have much higher artistic and aesthetic value than most run-of-the-mill paintings, even those by educated, professional artists.

Traditional aesthetic theory looks upon craft as a kind of exception or odd man out in the aesthetic field. In many ways, it is rather the fine arts that are the exception – and not only in the sense of the exceptionally refined. One may indeed argue that the fine arts were emancipated from the constraints of the older European, craft-dominated guild system of the Middle Ages, but that also means that they, to a certain extent, turned their backs on all the cultural values that we appreciate in the work of the talented and well-trained artisan: skilfulness, functionality and often also the special kind of function that we call embellishment. On the other hand, when paintings and sculptures are not cooped up in museums of fine art all over the world, but hang on the walls in people's homes, in offices and in private or public institutions, or are seen as statues and memorials in public places, do they not take on the virtues of adornment and social function that used to be considered as the prerogatives of craft?

Does this also mean that we can turn the tables completely and not see craft as the Other of the fine arts, but instead see the fine arts as the Other of craft? Not completely (hence the question mark after the title of the essay). The fine arts are not a shadowy Mr. Hyde to the skilful craftsperson, not a menace – but certainly a temptation. And if not the Other, then at least the odd man out.

Michael Rowe: *Cylindrical Vessel*, 1985. In the collection of the
National Museum of Art, Architecture and Design, Norway.
Photo: the National Museum of Art, Architecture and Design/
Frode Larsen

You In Between: From Aesthetic Difference to Aesthetic Differing

Knut Astrup Bull

Sculpture or container?

Some time ago, I had a discussion with a curator of contemporary art regarding Michael Rowe's *Cylindrical Vessel* from 1985 (Fig. 1). The object reminded the curator of sculptures from the 1960s, the implication being that it represented a bygone stage in art history. Even though there are of course several approaches to reading and experiencing works of contemporary craft, my response was nevertheless to point out that this was not *necessarily* a sculpture (re-presentation), but a vessel. The artist's intention was to present, from a formal, aesthetic and historical perspective, a conceptualization of a vessel meant to contain something. Rowe's vessel, I argued, should therefore not be seen only as a picturing (idea) of a container, or only as a container, but as a conceptual elaboration on the container (a thing) as a meaning-containing and complex object.

This discussion reveals a basic principle in the contemporary art discourse, namely, the oppositional relation between artworks, which, in the widest sense, depict or reflect reality, and ordinary things, which are part of the reality the artworks depict or reflect.[1] This antithetical conceptual pair, or the duality between art and objects used in everyday life, represents a dominating dogma undergirding and steering our perception and valuing of aesthetic objects, disqualifying some from being considered works of art. It also undergirds the institutional practice of ranking forms of art and positioning contemporary craft as

---

1   Even when artworks do not reflect reality, that is, when they do not act as images of everyday life, they are still seen as autonomous.

lower than (pictorial) art.[2] This aspect of the reigning aesthetic makes it difficult to see some works as 'both–and'; it nourishes a pattern of perception that categorizes objects as either art, or not.

In recent years, however, the epistemologies of (Post)modernity have become objects of critical analysis.[3] This is because it can be claimed that the patterns of perception emanating from dualist structures result in limiting our access to aesthetic objects and the status they are given. (Post)modernity's aesthetics are consistently dominated by conceptual contrasts that entice us to define objects based on what they are *not*, rather than what they are. In the discussion mentioned above, *Cylindrical Vessel* was the object of negative reflection on account of its qualities. The curator defined the object according to the qualities it lacked as an artwork; it was deemed retarded art, or it could be defined as an artwork only by ignoring certain 'unfitting' qualities.

Today's art discourse is still dominated by an aesthetic philosophy that springs from an idealistic tradition, the dualist commitments of which cause people to differentiate between art and the objects of everyday life. One consequence of this is to see (pictorial) art as antithetical to contemporary craft. In this article, I interpret the ceramic artist Anders Ruhwald's installation *You In Between* from 2008 (Fig. 2) as problematizing the dualism that partly marks the common perception and categorization of aesthetic objects. I look at how dualism gives guidelines for seeing a work as either art or craft, and how the judgment influences the way the work is interpreted. Based on Ruhwald's background as a craft artist and ceramist working in the expanded field of art, I will argue that it is relevant to interpret his installation as a reflection on dualism's tendency to reduce the perception of aesthetic objects. This dualism is particularly consequential for craft-based works, which are often seen as either 'picturing' objects, if they are accepted as artworks, or as functional objects that lack certain qualities of artworks. In the reigning art discourse, it is difficult to categorize objects that position themselves *in-between* the two opposing categories 'the depiction' and 'that which is depicted'. In my interpretation of *You In Between*, I see it as challenging the dualism of (Post)modernity.

---

2 I put 'pictorial' in parentheses in order to stress that the contemporary concept of art is a perpetuation of the concept of pictorial art.

3 In an epistemological sense, Postmodernity does not distinguish itself from the discourse of Modernity.

When we as viewers are placed in-between and amongst the objects that are placed in-between the antithetical categories of art and craft, the 'natural' mechanisms for categorization and classification are tested. Ruhwald, in this way, exposes the dualism and makes us aware of how the dichotomy steers perception and how it influences the relation between the art forms. It could be argued that Ruhwald wants to open up for a new reading of aesthetic objects, for how we view them in relation to each other and how we view the contrasting conceptual pairs they represent. If this is the case, it is fruitful to interpret *You In between* as a New-materialist reflexive analysis of the art discourse's dualistic pattern of perception. New-materialism analyses systems of thought that are built on dualism and aims to expose their limitations. I argue that Ruhwald, by using a New-materialist strategy, gives us the opportunity to discover how we structure our reading of objects based on contrasting conceptual pairs. We are thus challenged to see objects without letting our perception be restricted by dualism. It also becomes possible to glimpse the connection between the art forms – a connection that dualism obscures. Instead of allowing the differences to appear as negative or opposing relationships, Ruhwald promotes a perception that affirms the differences. The installation facilitates a pattern of perception that sees kinship between the artwork and craft, rather than looking for their opposing qualities. The installation also makes us aware of the opportunity to view works of contemporary craft as independent of the antithetical concepts.

After describing *You In Between*, I will read the installation as a New-materialist analysis of (Post)modernism's dualism and how it influences our categorization of aesthetic objects and what that entails. I will emphasize the impact of dualism on the relationship between craft and (pictorial) art. Furthermore, I will show how Ruhwald's installation facilitates a reading of craft that transcends the dichotomy of artworks/everyday objects. At the end of the article, I return to Rowe's *Cylindrical Vessel* and expand my reading of it based on the interpretive experience of Ruhwald's work.

You In Between

The installation *You In Between* is mounted in in the middle of a rectangular room with a yellow floor. The work stretches from wall to wall horizontally, and both ends of the room are left open. Two 'curtains' made of light blue silk ribbon divide the room horizontally. Between

Anders Ruhwald: *You in Between*, 2008. Exhibited at Middelsbrough institute of Modern Art, 2008. In the collection of the National Museum of Art, Architecture and Design, Oslo. Photo: Anders Ruhwald

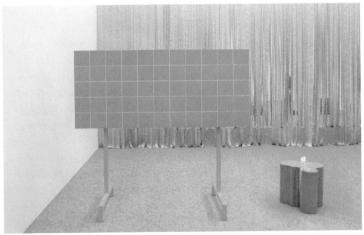

these room dividers is an in-between space, about two metres wide. On each outer side of this middle space, there are seven objects placed in a row. Every second object has either a light blue or an orange glaze. What differentiates one row of objects from the other row is the surface quality. One row of objects has a smooth and industrial surface, while the other has a rough surface, seemingly marked by a ceramist's fingers. Each object stands opposite its twin on the far side of the curtains and has the opposite glaze colour. For example, a smooth-surfaced panel of orange tiles stands in contrast to a rough-surfaced light blue panel of tiles. The way the installation is composed makes it impossible for us as viewers to gain a complete overview, regardless of where we stand in the room. It is possible to glimpse the objects on the far side of the silk ribbons but impossible to see them in their entirety. We must move back and forth to form an impression of the installation as a whole.

What kind of objects has Ruhwald placed on either side of the silk-ribbon room dividers? Several of them seem to be based on objects of use – for instance, a chalkboard, a stool, a table for holding an object such as a candlestick – but for other objects, it is difficult to imagine what their point of origin might be. Perhaps they are merely the result of formal experiments. One aspect shared by all the objects is abstraction. This also imbues them with sculptural qualities. But it is impossible to decide conclusively whether they should be interpreted as manipulated functional objects or as sculptures. The objects can thus be characterized as hybrids, in a category in-between privileged autonomous art and the functional objects of everyday life. It is this condition of undecidability that we also find ourselves in. It is problematic to categorize the objects by using dualism's pattern of perception. Are these sculptures or hip designer objects, or should they be viewed as conceptual works of craft – and if the latter is the case, the objects can indeed be subsumed under a more general category – but which one? Ruhwald, it seems, has deliberately created objects that position themselves in-between the aesthetic categories of pictorial art, craft and design. As viewers, we find ourselves in a fluctuating and indeterminate situation, one where the conventional patterns of perception based on contrasting conceptual pairs cannot definitively categorize the objects. With this installation, Ruhwald challenges a pattern of perception that is deeply rooted in (Post)modernity's aesthetic gaze, so much so that we see it as a 'natural' mode of viewing and evaluating art.

This is why the established pattern of perception (the division between art and ordinary things) is seldom an object for critical reflection in the art discourse. It is taken for granted as a precondition. What, then, are the historical discursive conditions underpinning this 'natural' pattern of perception that creates a dichotomy between art and functional objects, or between craft-based art and (pictorial) art?

Dualism in (Post)modernity's art discourses

We have touched on a well-known principle in the twentieth century's idealist-influenced art discourse, namely, the marked distinction between a picture and what it depicts. There is, in the Norwegian context, a by-now dogeared historical reference in art polemics: the poet Stein Mehren's criticism in the 1970s of craft artists' demand to have their works be seen as art.[4] In the tradition of predecessors such as Adolf Loos,[5] Le Corbusier[6] and others, Mehren claimed that a healthy, modern and stable culture is dependent on there being a clear distinction between works of art and craft-based functional objects. In this duality, an artwork transcends itself and points beyond its physical thing-ness. It reflects and comments on everyday reality from an autonomous position – it is a *depiction*. The craft-based work (the object of use), meanwhile, does not point to anything beyond itself or its own form – it only *pictures itself*. To upset this dualism, claimed Mehren, was to create cultural turmoil. The conceptual contrast between picturing something other than oneself and self-picturing is a dualism that continues to dominate the perception of art, even though the contrast does not appear as clearly in today's discourses as it did during High Modernism.[7] This internalized pattern of perception is undoubtedly a challenge for contemporary craft artists, who, through their ideation

4   Stein Mehren, 'Kunstverket og kunsthåndverket mellom en faktasivilisasjon og en opplevelseskultur', *Essays 50/60/70/80* (Oslo: Aschehoug, 1980).

5   Adolf Loos, 'Ornament and Crime', in *Programs and Manifestoes on 20th-Century Architecture*, ed. Ulrich Conrad, (Cambridge, MA: MIT Press, 1971), 19–24.

6   Le Corbusier, *The Decorative Art of Today* (London: The Architectural Press, 1987), 83–105.

7   See, for example, Nicolas Bourriaud's discussion on relational form, in which the work of art is described as to open up for an alternative reality (dialogue) alongside of everyday life. Bourriaud, *Relational Aesthetics* (Dijon: les presses du reel), 11–24.

and practice, often thematically address and problematize object-fixated culture, techniques, materials and social conditions. The spur for their activity is not *necessarily* to reflect reality from an autonomous position; historically speaking, they work in a materialistic tradition that is not undergirded by the concept of autonomy. Their works are often *specific* objects (in a material sense) that invite aesthetic reflection and experiences of realization within material reality – they do not transcend it. As such, some types of contemporary craft are in conflict with the dualism of the art discourse inasmuch as they picture themselves simultaneously as they depict something beyond themselves. *You In Between*, with its ambivalent objects, seems to cut across the established oppositional conceptual pairs. It is therefore fruitful to read the work into a New-materialist strategy for visualizing (Post)modernity's aesthetic dichotomies, given how it challenges the tendency of the art discourse to categorize craft-related works either as functional objects (self-picturing) or as artworks (depictions of something else). We can also read the installation as a statement about establishing a less-polarized perception of art objects in general and craft-based works in particular.

New-materialism: A reflection on antithetical concepts

There are of course several approaches to New-materialism and how its perspectives on describing phenomena can be used. One example is to follow Elisabeth Grosz in viewing art as not only the fruit of a rational process, but also as springing from biology. She expresses an understanding of art that weaves together culture and nature. Since her analysis is not steered by the contrast between a subject and object, it can be linked to a form of New-materialism.[8] As the term implies, New-materialism springs from a Materialist philosophical tradition. The adjective 'new' refers to *a reading* of texts that emancipates itself from epistemologies and philosophical traditions. But the reading is based on a materialist perspective that is critical towards (Post)modernity's dichotomies and concept-oriented prioritizations that prize rationality more than material manifestations. The relatedness to Materialism lies in giving the object a position that is more equal to

---

8   Elisabeth Grosz, *Chaos, Territory, Art: Deleuze and the Framing of the Earth* (New York: Columbia University Press, 2008).

that of the subject; this happens through doing a reading of the subject/object relation in a way that rejects the value system of (Post)modernity.[9] The work *You In Between*, according to my interpretation, highlights dualism's impact on how we evaluate art. Ruhwald challenges fundamental thought patterns that steer our aesthetic gaze. In this section, therefore, I will link my understanding of New-materialism to Rick Dolphijn and Iris van der Tuin's book *New Materialism: Interviews and Cartographies*, which presents New-materialism as a reflection on thought patterns built on opposing conceptual pairs, or dualism.

New-materialism, according to Dolphijn and Tuin, can be described as a strategy aimed at exposing (Post)modernity's dualistic thought patterns and for reflecting over its opposing conceptual pairs and conceptual priorities.[10] The strategy for avoiding being captured by dualism is to read texts in a way that traverses epistemological systems. The goal for applying this approach to historical and contemporary texts and epistemologies is to seek a new platform for understanding constellations of issues and concepts without pitting them *against* each other. New-materialism is thus a form of analysis that does not necessarily try to falsify dualism; rather, it is a radical way of questioning the logic undergirding (Post)modernism's dialectic and dichotomies.[11] In other words, New-materialism involves a new way of reading and analysing texts and propositions. It is a rewriting of Modernity that avoids dualism at the same time as it preserves the differences between concepts.

The first project for New-materialism is to expose the limitations of dualism in order to elucidate the relation between concepts and phenomena. Dualism's limitations are its thought systems, which are built on conceptual pairs rooted in subject-object oppositions. For example, there is the opposition between culture (subject) and nature (object). In thought systems of this kind, a 'negative confirmation' of the concepts is presupposed and therefore establishes the opposition. The concepts are defined by what they are *not*, rather than what they *are*. This means they are presented as negative reflections of each other. The one concept becomes a negative confirmation of the other, and

---

9   Ibid., 151.
10   Rick Dolphijn and Iris van der Tuin, *New Materialism: Interviews and Cartographies* (Ann Arbor: Open Humanities Press/University of Michigan, 2012), 115.
11   Ibid., 100.

in reality, they thereby appear as one and the same concept. Culture represents the opposite of nature, and nature represents the opposite of culture. The philosopher Michel Serres summarizes the circularity of these types of conceptual oppositions: 'An idea opposed to another idea is always the same idea, albeit affected by the negative sign.'[12]

In other words, the different concepts remain unified as one and the same concept within a dualistic discourse. Similarly, in the (pictorial) art discourse, the work of craft and the work of art are the same concept in the sense that the craft represents what the art is not, and vice versa.

According to New-materialism, it is limiting to define a phenomenon based on what it is not, precisely because seeing the concepts as different becomes a hindrance. We end up occluding the relation between them, and they only appear as opposites. This is the logic of dualism, and it steers our categories of aesthetic objects, among other things. The goal of New-materialism is therefore to expose the negative relation in order to step out of dualism and focus instead on a positive confirmation of the differences.[13]

The positive confirmation of differences consists in not allowing ourselves to be steered by dualism's presupposed negative relations between concepts, for instance between art (pictorial art) and everyday objects (craft). Nor is it a matter of upturning dualism's value system by giving materiality (object) precedence over the idea (subject).[14] By conceptualizing the negative relation, New-materialism pushes dualism to an extreme– it becomes glaringly obvious – and the opportunity arises to re-write Modernity by cutting across time and epistemological systems.[15] We land in a position where we can see the relation between the oppositional concepts in a new and affirming way. A space opens up for seeking connections rather than oppositions. New-materialism can thus be seen as a reflection over and a conceptualization of conceptual differences.[16]

---

12 Ibid., 120.
13 Ibid., 121.
14 Ibid., 115.
15 Ibid., 124.
16 Ibid., 119.

Ruhwald's artistic strategy in the installation *You In Between* is to make it difficult to categorize the objects according to contrasting concepts. This strategy can be interpreted as an exposure of the dualism underlying the art institution's dominating pattern of perception. When we as viewers have problems categorizing the objects, we are forced to reflect on the criteria we use for interpretation. In this way, Ruhwald challenges our perception of objects based on polarizing the artwork and the works of contemporary craft (whether it is functional or not). We cannot avoid feeling that something is lost when we try to establish opposing concepts by subsuming them under the one or the other category of objects. When it becomes problematic to read the objects, we must search for other contexts for understanding them. We are driven to look for connections in-between object categories rather than to define them based on what they are *not*. Ruhwald's work thus push dualism to its utmost, and we as viewers can reflect over the differences and the limitations and opportunities they represent.

Dualism's value system
As stated, *You In Between* 'forces' us to wander around in the work in order to form an overall picture of it. We must *get together* with the objects in a bodily way. This work activates a different form of viewing than what is normal in (Post)modernity's patterns of perception, which is to have a subject stand in a 'static' position and, on a purely conceptual level, to reflect on an artwork. In this traditional scenario, the transcendent subject is the locus for viewing, not the body. The transcendent viewer is thus in a prioritized position and has higher status than does material reality. Ruhwald challenges this value system when he makes us wander in-between the objects rather than viewing them from a fixed point. In so doing, he also gives the objects greater meaning. It is not only the objects' conceptual content that has aesthetic value, but also their physical presence as objects and how they activate our bodily experiences.[17] This aspect of *You In Between* can thus be interpreted as challenging dualism's value system, which focuses largely on intellectual rather than bodily experience.

---

17 This perspective is discussed in by Anders Ljungberg, in his article 'An Emotional Perspective on Everyday Use' in the present book.

Dualism represents a value system that involves giving definitions of concepts and phenomena negative meanings, such that one concept can be seen as superordinate to another. An example of such a fundamental dualism is the relation between a subject and an object, where the subject is often placed in a privileged position. This stems from the philosopher René Descartes' famous proposition '*Cogito ergo sum*'. Here it is only the transcendental subject, one who has the ability to reflect over (abstract) concepts that cannot be experienced, who is the guarantor for true knowledge. With this, an accentuated dualism was established in Western philosophy. Humanism's dualism has then created a marked distinction between the human being and the world, or between art and reality, as it were. Despite Postmodernity's acknowledgement of the radical limits of reason, dualism remains a basic structure in contemporary epistemologies.[18] As we have seen, objects are still categorized according to what they are not, and they are hierarchically valued along a subject-object axis. This is also how the dominating art discourse functions, one example being the oppositional relation between a work of contemporary craft and an artwork, where the former is linked to everyday reality (the object), while the artwork stands closer to a concept and the faculty of reason (the subject). Accordingly, the work of contemporary craft lands in a position of lower value than the pictorial work.

By challenging the pattern of perception resulting from the logic of dualism, *You In Between* also challenges the hierarchy in and between art institutions, where the transcendent art is deemed superior to the non-transcendent art – that is, craft-based art. By presenting objects that viewers have difficulty categorizing, it also becomes problematic when trying to categorize them according to a hierarchy of value. By this means, Ruhwald avoids participating in the part of the contemporary craft discourse that tries to 'elevate' craft to the status of 'fine' art by emphasizing its concept (idea) and ability to depict objects other than itself. He does not try to nudge craft towards the 'subject' end of the subject-object axis. There is a tendency in the discourse to write contemporary craft into a narrative of emancipation or to see it as participating in a developmental process that starts from the position

---

18 Dolphijn and Tuin, *New Materialism*, 110.

of functional objects and moves towards (pictorial) art.[19] When this happens, works of contemporary craft are actually being presented as belonging to a less valuable art form, or one which has been supressed by the domineering (pictorial) art. This side of the discourse has been about attributing certain qualities to the craft-based art form that resemble the qualities of (pictorial) art, in order to achieve equal status between the art forms. The consequence of this narrative and strategy is to erase the distinctive characteristics of craft. So we can rightly ask: Does such a discourse promote a genuine emancipation of craft art and equal status between the art forms, or does it undermine craft art?

From aesthetic difference to aesthetic differing

With respect to the relation between (pictorial) art and craft-based art; (Post)modernity's art discourse has, as far as craft art is concerned, been marked by a striving to overcome dualism by giving craft art the same characteristics as (pictorial) art. In this way, it should be possible to categorize craft art within the dominant art concept and achieve equal status for the art form. The strategy, however, only confirms dualism and the oppositional relation. What is more, with this strategy, there is a risk of transforming craft art into pictorial art rather than giving the forms of art equal status. Parts of the contemporary craft art discourse therefore represent a dilemma. The arguments giving works of contemporary craft the status of (pictorial) art implicitly confirm craft art's subordinate position. The discourse highlights the injustice of craft art's subordinate role and seeks to eliminate the difference on behalf of craft art, which can also be seen as a product of the (pictorial) art discourse's dominance within art institutions. Paradoxically, it is this part of the craft art discourse that contributes to entrenching precisely the difference it wants to erase.[20] The discourse remains within the logic of dualism where, in reality, craft art and (pictorial) art are the same concept 'albeit affected by the negative sign', as Serres put it. We place the art form into a system in which an object must either be called an artwork or a functional object, and we end up limiting our opportunity to have a flexible and potent concept of craft art.

---

19 This strategy is well illustrated in a book by Gunnar Danbolt, *From Bowl to Art – Arne Åse and Modern Norwegian Ceramics* (Stavanger: Dreyer, 1994).
20 Dolphijn and Tuin, *New Materialism*, 133.

The only outcome of such a strategy has been the coining of the concept *material-based art*, which in actual fact cannot distinguish works of craft from works made with any other media for which materials and skill are considered important, such as painting and classic sculpture. There is, however, no doubt that craft art is a full-value art form, and that there is an obvious kinship between craft art and (pictorial) art. I interpret Ruhwald's intension as being to promote an alternative story of emancipation (emancipation from dualism), where craft art's historical preconditions are retained at the same time as contemporary craft art can continuously emerge and have opportunities and relationships with 'ordinary' things as well as with (pictorial) art. Maybe it is this that Ruhwald implies by presenting objects that have characteristics of both art forms. To emphasize a craft object's qualities is to be concrete and conceptual *simultaneously*. The idea is a reflection over the object, and the object is a materialization of the idea about the object.[21] Instead of dualism, New-materialism promotes a *monistic* perspective,[22] thus making it possible to see the connections between concepts. The craft work and the pictorial work represent different forms of art, but they are still close kin. Perhaps *You In Between* points to a situation of standing in-between the conventional contrasting conceptual pair. Reading it in this way, Ruhwald's work represents a shift in the discourse – *from* focusing on difference (oppositions) *to* focusing on being aesthetically differing (different), and thereby not reducing craft art to either depiction or self-picturing.[23]

Perception in a New-materialist perspective

You In Between can be interpreted as problematizing a key point in Modernity's aesthetics: the contrast between a (pictorial) artwork and an object common to the everyday sphere (a work of craft). The artwork is dependent on being separate from and superior to the crafted and functional thing, just as theory is separate from and hierarchically superior to get-your-hands-dirty practice in (Post)modernity's dualist aesthetics.

---

21 Ibid., 151.

22 A recurring theme in much of New-materialism's reflections is Benedictus de Spinoza's *monism*. Being a critic of René Descartes' dualism, Spinoza himself argued for a double-aspect theory that aimed to see all of existence as belonging to the same substance.

23 Dolphijn and Tuin, *New Materialism*, 121.

The dichotomies constitute the hub of the patterns of perception emanating from an idealist aesthetic. The crafted object often stands in opposition to the art discourse's distinction between an artwork and an object of use. But by simultaneously being both an aesthetic object and an 'ordinary' thing, it can be claimed that the work of contemporary craft has a *transversal* character: it cuts across the dichotomy of art and everyday things and thereby places itself in a difficult aesthetic position. It is neither an ordinary thing nor a pure artwork, so it appears as an 'unclean' art form with low status in a dualistically based art discourse.

Ruhwald does not appear to pass judgment on which pattern of perception takes precedence or has more value than any other. In *You In Between*, it appears that perception switches back and forth between several viewing alternatives. I choose nevertheless to interpret the intention behind the work as being to lead us towards a pattern of perception that can be linked to a materialist aesthetic tradition. After all, the work makes us aware of aspects of craft from the past and the present that stand in opposition to dualism's categorical division between autonomous aesthetic objects and 'ordinary' things. Historically, what we today refer to as craft art has stood in opposition to the duality between art and everyday reality, and it has been, and remains, a form of art that has elements of the conceptual and the concrete, as we have seen. With *You In Between*, Ruhwald reveals contemporary craft's position, which Louise Mazanti describes as semi-autonomous.[24] She points out that contemporary craft operates 'within the gallery' and therefore has withdrawn from everyday reality, but at the same time *does not* link itself to an autonomous aesthetic. It insists on keeping the craft-based work of art in everyday life. This work is simultaneously conceptual and concrete, simultaneously an artwork and an ordinary thing. It is a specific thing that opens up for reflection on the thing in itself and the relations and contexts that the thing is a part of in our material and immaterial culture. And so it is with Ruhwald's work: it invites a New-materialist reading of the relation between the artwork, the craft-based work and the thing. *You In Between* reaffirms craft-based art's origin in the Materialist aesthetic tradition, which sought to avoid dualism's limitations in the aesthetic sphere.

---

24 Louise Mazanti, *Superobjekter: En teori om det nutidig, konseptuelt kunsthåndværk*. Ph.D. dissertation, Danmarks designskole (Copenhagen, 2006), 206.

The Materialist avant-garde

The Arts and Crafts Movement represented an ideological revolt against the idealist aesthetics that were on the verge of achieving hegemony in the late nineteenth century. The movement was not a small group of artists linking themselves to one manifesto; it consisted of artists, artist groups and theorists who shared similar views on debates concerning contemporaneous art and society. One similarity between the tone-setting writers was that they advocated for an aesthetic inspired by the philosophy of Karl Marx. This is evident from William Morris's texts written during 1877–96,[25] and from Walter Crane's book *The Claims of Decorative Art,* first published in 1891.[26] Both authors argue for a new art that contradicts the distinction between art and everyday life. For them, the dichotomy introduced by autonomous art is a symptom of art's absence from everyday life in an industrialized society. They turn away from the aesthetics of idealist philosophy and towards a materialist philosophical tradition that rejects the distinction between subject and object, which they see as a philosophical construction. Their view harmonizes with that of Marx.[27] Marx's starting assumption is that the faculty of reason and the body are two sides of the same coin, as it were, hence reason (art) cannot transcend the everyday sphere. It could be that Marx draws inspiration from a statement by Spinoza: 'Being the mind is an idea of the body, while the body is the object of the mind.'[28]

From such a perspective, art does not stand outside everyday reality, but constitutes it through a reconciliation between the subject and object within the everyday framework. In this way, the Materialist aesthetic sets aside dualism in art. The Arts and Crafts Movement's aesthetic, read through Morris and Crane, dissolves the boundary between art and everyday life, but at the same time, a new dichotomy emerges within the institution of art, namely, the distinction between pictorial art and craft, or between autonomous and non-autonomous art.

---

25 William Morris, 'Art under Plutocracy', in *William Morris – On Art and Socialism*, ed. Norman Kelvin (New York: Dover, 1999), 108–128.

26 Walter Crane, *The Claims of Decorative Art* (Milton Keynes UK: Bibliolife, 2009).

27 Terry Eagleton, *The Ideology of the Aesthetic* (Oxford: Blackwell, 1990), 201.

28 Dolphijn and Tuin, *New Materialism*, 151.

Ruhwald, for his part, dissolves the antagonism between the concepts 'artwork' and 'work of craft' that was established by Materialist aesthetics. Through *You In Between*, he does a new reading of Materialism in light of his own era's craft discourse and challenges dualism through exposing the limitations of seeing a (pictorial) artwork and a work of contemporary craft as opposites. His installation implies instead that the art forms should be seen simply as *different*. In contrast to the part of the discourse that wants to attribute the same qualities to the craft-based work as those common to the (pictorial) work (the aesthetics of dualism), he chooses instead to acknowledge the history of his art form: the past and future of craft meet in the work here and now. *You In Between* liberates the Materialist aesthetic from the art/craft dichotomy through a reading that cuts across time and aesthetic thought systems. The installation brings the discourse and the relation between craft and art to the point where it can reject aesthetic *oppositions* and embrace aesthetic *differences*. Instead of appearing as a negative reflection of each other, he moves the discourse towards a positive confirmation of the differences between them. With this strategy, craft art can be read from the perspective of an independent aesthetic position freed from the dichotomy. It is given the possibility to operate in the space in-between them. Ruhwald gives us the opportunity to view craft art without letting it be limited by the dichotomy.

Closing thoughts

There are several ways to approach Michael Rowe's *Cylindrical Vessel*, and each one offers meaning. The work can be seen as a sculpture or as a container that has been given some kind of treatment. Our reflection on Ruhwald's work and on opposing conceptual pairs, however, has revealed the limitations of categorizing a work according to a dualist paradigm. This revelation gives us the possibility of seeing a work such as *Cylindrical Vessel* as a monistic aesthetic object – one in which the idea of the object represents a reflection on the vessel *per se*, and the vessel we see is a materialization of the idea about the concept of the vessel. This work can therefore be interpreted as a transversal object un-chained from the dichotomy of the artwork and the functional object. It operates in the space between the antithetical positions. If we are to see the full potential of an object, we must see the kinship between the artwork and the craft-based work. The similarity and the difference between the two must be confirmed in a positive way through accepting the crafted work's conceptual and concrete or specific qualities on their own terms. Only then will the conditions be right for equality between the art forms, and only then will we see an object like Rowe's *Cylindrical Vessel* as an idea and a container at *one and the same* time. Only then will we not be faced with the choice of either seeing it as a sculpture or as a functional object. Anders Ruhwald's *You In Between*, interpreted from a New-materialist perspective, represents a new reading of the craft work's materialistic aesthetic and provides the foundation for a form of perception that unleashes the full aesthetic potential of craft art.

A Widening Chromaticism:
Learning Perception
in the Collective Craftwork
of the Encounter

Sarah R. Gilbert

Crafty Ants Form Conga Lines to Drag Millipedes to Doom.
– Matt Simon, *Wired.com*

The click-bait, in this case, does not disappoint. An embedded video shows a swarm of ants encircling and stinging a single large millipede as it thrashes in and out of defensive recoil. The millipede weighs-in at more than a thousand times the weight of an individual ant, and the collective efficacy of the swarm is breathtakingly, terrifyingly, powerful. But the most extraordinary moment comes, not with this climactic attack sequence, but in the dénouement: instead of the ants grabbing each their own part of the millipede as they move to drag it, now paralyzed, back to their nest, the ants form 'self-assembling chains.'[1] One ant grabs hold of a millipede leg or antenna, while a second ant connects to that ant's abdomen, and so on, with as many as twenty ants coordinating their movements into linear linkages of *pull*. Sometimes two or three of these linked chains form simultaneously in parallel. Sometimes these linear chains become branching chains, as two or three ants start new linkages off of the same ant's abdomen at various points down the line. Even as the overall assemblage pulls towards the nest, some of the ants are pushing or lifting, reducing friction or clearing paths. The chains appear both precisely ordered and strikingly dynamic, frequently dissolving and reforming anew in response to particular obstacles of terrain encountered en route.

---

1   Christian Peeters and Stephane De Greef, 'Predation on Large Millipedes and Self-assembling Chains in Leptogenys Ants from Cambodia', *Insectes Sociaux,* vol. 62, no. 4 (2015), 471–477.

Following craft theorist Glenn Adamson's important call to approach craft as a *verb*, rather than a *noun*, we might consider the 'crafty' movements of these *Leptogenys* ants as skilled labour in the service of specific ends: oriented towards the shared purpose of securing food, they are able to become a kind of collective super-organism, significantly more capable than the sum of their parts. As a verb describing human activity, craft likewise tends to evoke collective and repetitive labour, oriented towards predetermined ends. No matter how inspired someone is in the moment, a well-crafted wooden table, for example, can't just be made on the fly. Hand-skills must be learnt through repeated practice over time, until they become internalized as muscle-memory or 'second nature'. Order-of-operations are imperative to joinery, so construction must also be known in advance. Many practitioners share the same techniques, and these develop, not only over the lifetime of an individual woodworker, but also across the wider practice and deeper histories of the craft itself.

Since wilful individual action and novel production are often positioned as the very defining qualities of human culture, the question of what exactly *changes* in craft can quickly become deeply troubling. If art evokes all the experimental sexiness of the avant-gardes, and design all the enterprising invention of modern production, craft more often conjures naïve or reactionary conservatism. To contest such conservatism, Adamson highlights craft's crucial 'supplemental' role within the relatively autonomous field of modern and contemporary art, while also challenging functional object-makers to more self-consciously deploy craft as a critical practice within the visual arts as a whole.[2] In a kind of mirrored approach, sociologist Richard Sennett approaches the functional (or non-autonomous) dimension of craft as its primary strength, analysing innovative practices across woodshops, fab-labs, and architecture studios that emphasize the ethical implications of skilled labour as a means of self-reflectively anchoring people to reality and allowing them to take pride in their work.[3] While these insights have crucially expanded the scope and rigor of recent craft theory, framings of autonomy and function risk subsuming craft – especially the verb formation, *to craft* – within other practices, most

---

2   Glenn Adamson, *Thinking Through Craft* (London: Berg, 2007).

3   Richard Sennett, *The Craftsman* (New Haven: Yale, 2008).

notably art and design. This risk is compounded by a wider tendency to focus theories of craft perception on questions of maker intent, foreclosing in advance more distributed and relational approaches to agency and affect.

Skilled at pattern recognition and equipped with sophisticated apparatuses of scientific observation, researchers note that *Leptogenys* repeat the same crafty behaviour over and over: they form self-assembling chains in order to transport their prey. But every actual event – the specific movements and shifting choreography of these 'conga lines' as they unfold in real time and space – is also different, and radically contingent. *Leptogenys* don't simply *know* how, or *see* where to go (indeed, they usually face backwards while in these linkages), but instead *learn* how and where to go, as they go, together. *To craft*, then, requires navigating the material world through concrete experience in both major valences of the term, attentively experiencing the lived encounter as it unfolds, and also accruing experience through experimental trial and error.

The swarm moves through a multitude of complex negotiations within changing particulars on the ground, in a thousand collisions of various bits and pieces of ant, millipede, dirt, chemical trails, moisture, heat, etc. We couldn't actually 'sum' the capacities of these 'parts' if we wanted to, because we could never convincingly separate out all of the individual parts, let alone capacities, involved in such an event. The very phrase 'sum of their parts' only points to inadequacies in our language of individual/collective for articulating complex forms of relation, attention and attunement. Still, four other ant subfamilies are also known to form self-assembling chains, yet these do so specifically in the process of making objects, whether building rafts to survive flooding or moving leaves to construct nests.[4] So why begin an essay on craft with a story of insect predation?

---

4   Peeters and De Greef, 471. Also see Anderson, Theraulaz and Deneubourg, 'Self-assemblages in Insect Societies', *Insectes Sociaux*, vol. 49, no. 2 (2002), 99–110.

Most notably, *Leptogeny* point to the powerful potential of craft as a collective material practice irrespective of any finished object – functional or autonomous, novel or traditional – made in the process. What if, rather than assuming that the collective and repetitive aspects of craft are shortcomings to be surmounted, we instead explore them as vital aspects to craft, as a fecund practice for the cultivation of what the philosopher Gilles Deleuze calls 'the apprenticeship of the unconscious': a heightened corporeal attunement that opens material potential precisely by resisting any authorial 'I think' or 'I act' subject position?[5] *Leptogenys'* dynamic linkages highlight some limits to thinking of craft as the simple application of known means towards ends, and also suggest important affinities between craft-making and craft-perception.

Instead of approaching making and perception as two wholly distinct types of wilful individual action – the craftsman imposing form onto matter through the production of a crafted object, and the viewer perceiving and judging this fixed crafted object – we might consider both as encounters within a wide spectrum of sensuous curiosity, haptic learning and skilled collective care. Craft perception would then become less of an evaluative project, and more of a generative one. The skills required would not be deconstructive or even critical, but precisely the generous and open comportment that might prove capable of resisting such tendencies. Most urgently, this would require that we reclaim craft – in perception as much as in making – as not only a supplemental verb, but also a distinct *practice*, and our obligation to actively struggle for.

---

5   Gilles Deleuze, *Difference and Repetition*, trans. Paul Patton
    (New York: Columbia University Press, 1994, original French 1968).

Feeling-thinking, or crafting collective encounters

> What other reason is there for writing than to be traitor to one's
> own reign, traitor to one's sex, to one's class, to one's majority?
> And to be a traitor to writing.
> – Gilles Deleuze and Claire Parnet, *Dialogues II*

If social insects demonstrate the potential power of collective attunement, analogized to human behaviour, they also raise the spectres of
complacently instrumentalized worker-bees and the destructive ter-
rors of the unthinking mob. Kant notoriously distinguished between
our pleasure in perceiving the instinctively 'purposive' constructions
of honeybees, in contrast to the rational deliberation and freewill manifest in both the work of art's 'purposiveness without a purpose' and
our 'disinterested' perception of art in judgments of beauty:

> By right it is only production through freedom, i.e. through an act of will that
> places reason as the basis of its action, that should be called art. For, although
> we are pleased to call what bees produce (their regularly produced cells) a work
> of art, we only do so on the strength of an analogy with art; that is to say, as
> soon as we call to mind that no rational deliberation forms the basis of their
> labour, we say at once that is a product of their nature (of instinct), and it is
> only to their Creator that we ascribe it as art.[6]

The implications of such a paradigm for craft are pointedly noted by
craft theorist Howard Risatti, who goes so far as to blame the continuing denigration of craft as a supposedly anti-intellectual field relative
to art on 'Kant's division of the world of the man-made into two large
but unequal classes comprising the useful and the nonuseful'.[7] The
more functional the object, the more it seems compromised by natural instinct – less freely wilful, and so less human – in both its making
and its perception.

Since craft has so frequently been disparaged in comparison to art
– unreflectively collective to art's wilful individualism; conservatively
repetitious to art's experimental novelty; instrumentally functional to

---

6 Immanuel Kant, *The Critique of Judgment*, trans. J.H. Bernard
   (Oxford: Oxford University Press, 2008, original German 1790), 132.

7 Howard Risatti, *A Theory of Craft: Function and Aesthetic Form*
   (Chapel Hill: University of North Carolina Press, 2007), 217.

art's disinterested autonomy – efforts to elevate the former by ordaining it with the humanist authority of the latter understandably abound. Complementing the supplemental-verb strategies of Adamson and Sennett, Risatti importantly stakes out craft's necessary distinctiveness from both art and design by refocusing on craft objects. Drawing heavily from Kant, he defines craft as the abstract conceptualization of form, material, and technique intentionally applied to function, or as an intimately human and privileged subcategory of functional objects. While he sees craft objects as constitutively functional, they cannot – no matter how meticulously crafted – require, like cutlery or other tools, the 'input of kinetic energy' to 'activate them' or 'make them work'; they must be 'self-contained' or 'self-reliant'.[8] Vital contributions and major differences notwithstanding, craft theory framed in terms of function and autonomy tends to follow a similar grounding logic: for craft to be a meaningful practice it must be uniquely human, and so, to be distinguishable from the instinctively purposive behaviours of unthinking nature, it must either lay some supplemental claim to art's autonomous free-play of forms, or define craft's functional purposiveness as equally wilful and self-critically thoughtful to autonomous art.

But if this dialectic of function and autonomy concerns human culture, with nature only relevant as a foil against which humans define their distinctly free creativity, what kinds of craft-thinking might emerge if we, from the start, refuse this nature/culture binary and its implicit assumptions? For example, the assumption that craft must be the labour of individual human subjects who, by conscious reasoning and wilful action, transform inert material into the distinctly ingenious products of culture. Or the assumption that this inert material is extracted from a necessarily unconscious nature, composed of animals, vegetables, and minerals capable only of instinctual or deterministic behaviour. The problem with common-sense and what we call thought, Deleuze warns us, is that it tends to presuppose a self (someone *who* thinks), as well as 'good will on the part of the thinker and an upright nature on the part of thought'.[9] Taking for granted certain structuring categories and values – righteous human subjects,

---

8   Ibid., 46–47.

9   Deleuze, *Difference and Repetition*, 131.

applying their 'natural faculty' to recognize inherently noble truths – this habituated laziness of thinking effectively replaces God with modern Man, operating as a transcendent first principle that prohibits in advance any ideas which do not proceed in its image.

In contrast, Deleuze argues that thinking only happens *involuntarily*: 'Something in the world forces us to think.'[10] Emerging relationally, in all the contingencies of lived experience, thought can't be imagined, conceived of, or recalled, because it doesn't belong to, or emanate from, any single subject. It comes from the outside, and so can only be *sensed* or *felt*. Only in the encounter with something wholly unrecognizable, in all of its immediate sensuousness, can the 'claws of a strangeness or an enmity... awaken thought from its natural stupor'.[11] Thought is not the product of any subject's good-willed intentions, but rather *precisely the event in which our subjective categories and interpretive strategies fail.* Encounters with such sensations occur with some frequency to any serious woodworker, blacksmith, glassblower, weaver, etc. However, to open ourselves as vulnerably as possible to these sensations when walking around a craft museum, pouring our morning coffee, or snuggling under the covers, requires what the political theorist Jane Bennett calls a 'methodological naiveté...the postponement of a geneological critique of objects that might render manifest a subsistent world of nonhuman vitality'.[12]

As social insects make glaringly evident, what we call entities are not actually unitary and fixed beings, but rather heterogeneous and contingent concrescences of interpenetrating matter and forces. And, however much agency may seem to come from within, it also comes from without. A cow, for example, cannot complete even its most basic 'cowish' function – eating and digesting grass – without a multitude of genetically distinct microbial symbionts.[13] There's a concept in ecological developmental biology for this shifting and contextually actualizing assemblage: 'holobiont' replaces what we used to reductively

10 Ibid., 139.

11 Ibid.

12 Jane Bennett, *Vibrant Matter: A Political Ecology of Things* (Durham: Duke University Press, 2010).

13 Scott F. Gilbert and David Epel, *Ecological Developmental Biology: The Environmental Regulation of Development, Health, and Evolution*, 2nd ed. (Sunderland: Sinauer, 2015).

call 'organism'.[14] Even basic metabolism tells us that whatever 'I' am exists only by continuously changing its parts, and recent symbiosis theory takes this considerably further. I might call myself *Sarah*, but 'I' am not actually the same cells, the same matter, nor even the same collection of genetic material from one day to the next. Where we travel, what we eat, and every single material thing we come into contact with *matters*. These things change us – in ways both minor and major, pleasant and unpleasant – and our perception of the material world could only become richer the more fully we learn to experience this. Approaching agency as a distributed and relational phenomenon is not to suggest some boundless field of equally important actors for every event. On the contrary, it is to make both purpose and skill active questions within craft perception, instead of assuming human subjects and their intentional capacities in advance.

Craft and *crafty*, of course, are also not quite the same. While the former might evoke the dignified labour of skilled mastery, the latter implies a mischievous cleverness, or even treachery. Crafty is a warning: as Mike D. said, 'hide your gold, the girl is crafty like ice is cold!'[15] It's hardly surprising that the idea of noble craftsmanship tends to describe crafts*men*, while craftiness more often describes swarms of predatory ants and other suspiciously powerful creatures, including women ('girls') with little respect for private property, as well as many other humanities variously denied full entry into the category of Man.[16] And none of this, indeed, is actually a laughing matter, unless we acknowledge that even the very worst horrors can be. Consider the racialized classificatory system of Linnaeus' *Systema Naturae*, which described the African 'variety' of human as 'crafty, indolent, negligent', the 'women without shame. Mammae lactating profusely'.[17] *Crafty* marks transgressions against established order. Blasphemous laugher, when possible – and often, it is not – can be a powerful one.

---

14 Scott F. Gilbert, Jan Sapp, and Alfred I. Tauber, 'A Symbiotic View of Life: We Have Never Been Individuals', *The Quarterly Review of Biology*, vol. 87, no. 4 (2012), 325–341.

15 The Beastie Boys, 'She's Crafty', *Licensed to Ill* (New York: Def Jam, 1986).

16 On the project of thinking 'other humanities' within the problematic genealogy of received colonial and liberal humanism, see Lisa Lowe, *The Intimacies of Four Continents* (Durham: Duke University Press, 2015).

17 Carl Linnaeus, 1759, in James Slotkin, *Early Readings in Anthropology* (London: Routledge, 2011), 178.

.

To refuse to adapt one's body to the shape of this world's existing categories and structures is to become suspect: as queer feminist theorist Sara Ahmed incisively frames it, 'to create awkwardness is to be read as awkward'.[18] To do so shamelessly, in skilled liveliness with one's surroundings and without deference to one's indicated place within this established order, is to become a traitor. What might *craftier* theories of craft perception – theories in no way beholden to, or theories even openly traitorous to, Man's distinctive culture and its dialectic of function and autonomy – make possible?

---

18 Sara Ahmed, *The Promise of Happiness* (Durham: Duke University Press, 2010), 68.

Perceiving craft between a rock and a hard place

> No work of art within the organization of society can escape its involvement in culture but there is none, if it is more than mere handicraft, which does not make culture a dismissive gesture: that of having become a work of art.
> – Theodor Adorno, *Minima Moralia: Reflections from a Damaged Life*

Art and design are often seen, not simply as divergent, but as oppositional practices in the present. Function creates the primary division, determining primary criteria for design, while defining art in negation. Taken further, this division appears in blatantly ideological terms: art aims to critique dominant culture, while design continuously reproduces it.[19] Craft, as discussed above, tends to get caught in the middle, with contemporary art historians like John Roberts suggesting that skill itself must be redefined, as the honing of conceptual, rather than artisanal, labour.[20] As Adamson explores in *Thinking Through Craft*, Adorno's work offers a potent, if intuitively paradoxical, plea for autonomous art as a fundamentally political issue. Turning to our epigraph, we can see how the Kantian notion of disinterested beauty mutates within a certain continuing strain of mid-twentieth century critical theory to position autonomy as the unlikely criteria for cultural critique in the age of late capitalism.

Adorno wrote the collected aphorisms of *Minima Moralia* while in exile from Nazi Germany in the late 1940s, intertwining his experiences as a secular Jew displaced to Southern California with pithy and probing reflections on the many ways in which 'life does not live'[21] under the colluding technics of Enlightenment reason, fascism and the nation-state, and post-industrial consumer capitalism. In a society predicated on instrumentalizing all life and all things, the very *existence* of successful works of art – as simultaneously 'useless' objects, strong affective powers, and carriers of incongruous exchange value – exposes the arbitrary system of capitalist exchange and effectively

---

19 See especially Hal Foster, *Design and Crime (and other Diatribes)* (London: Verso, 2001).

20 John Roberts, *The Intangibilities of Form: Skill and Deskilling after the Readymade* (London: Verso, 2007).

21 This is the book's full and only epigraph, from the Viennese novelist Ferdinand Kürnberger.

puts culture-as-it-exists on trial. In so doing, art offers the possibility of something else: the fleeting glimpse of another possible world in which human labour and rich material matter might more freely associate. Art's political promise then lies, not in any content it might represent (as so doing would only reduce art to the function of propaganda), but rather in the messy dialectical tension produced by the artistic gesture itself – the labour made manifest without any immediate use. In the context of such a framework, 'mere handicraft' is an easy target. Against the status quo reproduction of more and more quotidian sameness, art seems to hold out as lone critical foil, promising novel possibilities for living.

Craft, as a practice distinct from both commercial design and critical art, is then made to carry a double burden: on the one hand, the tinkering hobbyist puttering about with unserious trifles and, on the other, the naïvely romantic studio craftsman, so proud to have gained control over the means of production, while pathetically reproducing very safe functional forms based on already-lived traditions. Similar formulations – and their attendant dismissiveness towards craft as a distinct practice – continue to be widespread, even (or especially) within craft discourse itself. In a 2015 interview with the *New York Times*, the director of the Smithsonian Institute's Renwick Gallery for American Craft, Elizabeth Broun, noted that while 'in the past, the museum might have shown the work of highly skilled artists toiling in isolation to create some exquisite object', in re-evaluating their mission on the occasion of the museum's grand re-opening, they wanted 'art that looks out'.[22] The exhibition, *Wonder*, traded the Renwick's former focus on crafted functional objects like pots and baskets for contemporary art – particularly large-scale, colourful installations that looked craft-*ish*, generally because of either the materials deployed, or because of a self-conscious approach to rendering the labour process easily visible.

At issue here is not the work in the exhibition, but rather its situatedness as the re-opening exhibition for such a notable institution dedicated to craft practice and, most especially, such a damaging statement on craft given by someone specifically entrusted to protect

---

22 Graham Bowley, 'Renwick Gallery Reopens with a New Focus',
    The New York Times, 12 November 2015.

it. There is, certainly, a well-known genealogy of heroic individualism and studio toil that can be constructed between the Victorian self-fashioning of the Arts and Crafts movement and the gestural self-expressivity of much of the American Studio Craft movement in the 1960s–90s; but to imply that this represents the lively field of crafted studio objects today or in recent history indicates either ignorance or prejudice. What, indeed, makes the highly 'interested' practices of so many hobbyists – those who have day jobs or who otherwise spend their days attending to others, often in and out of the studio creating objects as part of these embedded practices – so un-serious, besides this tired craft history repeatedly evoked by the gatekeepers of institutional rigor, only to highlight art's critical capacities in contrast? That craft is far more often anonymous and collective, as well as deeply enmeshed in the complexity of the world-at-large, is completely ignored in Broun's statement, while the unfashionable baggage of the individual artist in the studio is easily distanced from contemporary art practices and instead projected onto the crafted object's perceived retrograde conservatism.

And what exactly makes the studio, or crafted studio objects, so fundamentally conservative, especially in our current moment when many artists outsource messy material labour entirely? To prioritize craft as a verb does not require that we relegate objects to the category of safe convention; indeed, it might require approaching the crafting of objects outside the safe convention of any function/autonomy dialectic in which the supposedly free-play of art is always-already more complex and in need of exhibition or theoretical discourse.[23] It is not at all evident that the omission of crafted objects from an exhibition is 'less safe' than an exhibition made entirely of them. One could just as well argue the opposite: that large-scale, brightly coloured installations simply repeat the endless spectacle of keeping us all distracted and entertained, while relatively diminutive objects might incite more unexpected encounters, even if only by provoking some initial boredom.

---

23 'A modern object that ticks all the craft boxes... may be fascinating from the perspective of a historian, but it does not necessarily present an interesting case for theoretical discourse... to write those histories accurately, we must concede that they occupy a safe position in the landscape of the visual arts – a lagoon, perhaps.' Adamson, *Thinking Through Craft*, 169.

A studio practice can allow for the careful honing-in of specific material problems and, studio objects, likewise, often offer uniquely subtle openings for perceiving material intensities that would never otherwise be possible.

Installations, of course, are also not somehow exempt from the category of nouns. To seriously approach craft as a verb requires us to acknowledge – not only that very traditional practices of functional object-making can sometimes become highly subversive, and that relatively autonomous practices of installation art can sometimes become highly conservative – but also that the function/autonomy dialectic forces out many vibrant material practices that produce no nouns whatsoever. As engineering professor Debbie Chachra notes in 'Why I am Not a Maker', her delightfully apostatical critique of contemporary tech culture and the maker movement: 'It's not, of course, that there's anything wrong with making (although it's not at all clear that the world needs more stuff). The problem is the idea that the alternative to making is usually not doing nothing.'[24] The alternative is, more often than not, various practices of devalued maintenance and care.

As we start to acknowledge and learn to navigate this Anthropocene epoch of irreversible human-driven climate change and mass species extinction, the absurdity of any clear separation between culture and nature could hardly be more evident. And when 99 percent of consumer products are no longer in use even six months after sale,[25] our distinctly human capacities seem to show less as any particularly thoughtful creativity, and more as the incessant privileging of 'innovative' production and growth at the expense of all else – indeed, at the expense of much life on earth. To approach craft as the collective craftwork of encounter is to focus, not on the uniquely human production of functional objects or autonomous installations, but rather on craft's potential for generating novel *experiences* – as much in perception as in production – through the skilful material practice of sensuous curiosity and collective care.

---

24 Debbie Chachra, 'Why I Am Not a Maker', *The Atlantic*, 23 January 2015.
25 Annie Leonard, *The Story of Stuff* (film), cited in George Monbiot, 'On the 12th Day of Christmas Your Gift Will Just Be Junk', *The Guardian*, 10 December 2012.

Practical matters

> A materialist conception of care needs to stay close to the implications of caring when giving marginalized things a voice in the staging of technoscientific mediations not only as a way of resisting to idealize care as a moral disposition, but also as a normative epistemic stance disconnected from the material doings that make the web of care in technoscience.
> (María Puig de la Bellacasa, *Matters of Care: Speculative Ethics in More than Human Worlds*)

Objects, however exquisitely crafted, are not uniquely complicit in the deforming and destructive logics of capitalist exchange, and it's time we stop rendering them the supposedly safe, conservative scapegoat. To accept a grant, teaching position, or curatorial post, or to receive any kind of press or award, is to be 'interested' and to include an object, installation, or any other creation within a constellation of functional concerns. Adorno was, indeed, well aware of this latter bit. Writing to his friend and colleague, Walter Benjamin, on the relationship between autonomous art and the easily consumed products of the culture industry, he notes:

> Both bear the stigmata of capitalism, both contain elements of change... Both are torn halves of an integral freedom, to which however they do not add up. It would be romantic to sacrifice one to the other, either as the bourgeois romanticism of the conservation of personality and all that stuff, or as the anarchistic romanticism of blind confidence in the spontaneous power of the proletariat in the historical process – a proletariat which is itself a product of bourgeois society.[26]

They are dialectical, and romanticizing the possibility of one without the other would be absurd. But this is also why Adorno's theory of autonomous art is so inextricable from his relentless critique of subjectivity, something far fewer craft theorists care to explore:

> No theory today escapes the marketplace. Each one is offered as a possibility among competing opinions; all are put up for choice; all are swallowed. There are no blinders for thought to don against this, and the self-righteous

---

26 Theodor Adorno, 'Letter to Walter Benjamin: 18 March 1936', *Aesthetics and Politics: The Key Texts of the Classic Debate within German Marxism*, ed. Ronald Taylor (London: Verso, 2002).

conviction that my own theory is spared that fate will surely deteriorate into self advertising.[27]

If, under capitalism, everyday commodities embody all the sensuous powers of human life, human life is equally rendered 'thingly' in the exchange: a deformed and mutilated shell, unaware and unable to enact its fully human potential. For Adorno, human freedom – for the artist at least as much as the studio craftsman – functions only as ideology. The power of artworks then emerges, not because of any self-conscious authorial intention, but in spite of it:

> Common sense, inclined to equate the spirit of artworks with what their makers infuse into them, must rapidly enough discover that artworks are so coconstructed by the opposition of the artistic material, by their own postulates, by historically contemporary models and procedures that are elemental to a spirit that may be called-in a condensed fashion that deviates from Hegel-objective, that their reduction to subjective spirit becomes absurd.[28]

If much of recent craft theory focuses on supplemental verbs and authorial intent to the exclusion of objects, Adorno's focus on the finished artwork and the 'preponderance of the object' is so strong that it tends to conflate practice with subjective intent, dismissing it as mere ideology.

As the philosopher of science Isabelle Stengers has widely argued, this suspicion of ideology points to an important shortcoming of Marxist criticism more generally: no practice, it warns, is ever what it seems, and no practitioners can be trusted; they always have something more to lose than their chains.[29] But while such critical analyses can be both intellectually satisfying and difficult to argue with, their insistent suspicion nonetheless leaves practices entirely vulnerable:

27 Theodor Adorno, *Negative Dialectics* (London: Continuum, 2005, original German 1966), 4.

28 Theodor W. Adorno, *Aesthetic Theory*, trans. Robert Hullot-Kentor (Minneapolis: University of Minnesota Press 1997, original German 1970), 345.

29 Isabelle Stengers, 'Wondering About Materialism', in *The Speculative Turn: Continental Realism and Materialism*, eds. Levi Bryant, Nick Srnicek, Graham Harman (Melbourne: re:press, 2011), 377.

> There is no practice the destruction of which cannot be justified, either by the privileges they benefited, or by their alienating archaism, or by their closure and resistance to change, but all those reasons, if they amount to justifying why destruction is not a cause for struggle, also amount to giving free elbow-room to capitalism in its ongoing destructive redefinition of the world.[30]

The issue with autonomy, then, is not that Adorno is mistaken in arguing that art, by carving out a space to resist the repressive logics of capitalism, can occasionally unfurl other potential worlds in the process. The point is, rather, that art is no more intrinsically capable of doing so than 'mere handicraft' – and certainly not by virtue of any isolation from practical concerns or the criteria of uselessness against reproduction of the status quo. Usefulness is a straw man; function does not equal instrumentality. To frame creative practice as a dialectic of function and autonomy is to artificially reduce practice to ideology, placing two mirrors in an infinite regress of comparative redefinition: all the differences are basically the same. Design can optimistically insist on its inherently useful obligation to keep producing things that serve practical purposes, while art smugly derides them to define itself as critical resistance. Either way, the theoretical richness of art and design practices are constrained in advance, and craft practice is invariably threatened in the process.

In a remarkable discussion of blacksmithing towards the end of one of their collaborative philosophical texts, *A Thousand Plateaus*, Deleuze and Guattari offer a materialist account of craft that inverts conventional perceptions of craft's conservatism. Metal, they note, is 'coextensive to the whole of matter... Even the waters, the grasses and varieties of wood, the animals are populated by salts or mineral elements'.[31] The skilled blacksmith, then, does not wilfully impose some abstractly-conceptualized form onto inert matter, but instead practices a kind of haptically conductive attunement with the material world at-large:

30 Ibid.

31 Gilles Deleuze and Félix Guattari, *A Thousand Plateaus: Capitalism and Schizophrenia*, translated by Brian Massumi (Minneapolis: University of Minnesota Press, 2005, original French 1980), 411.

Matter and form have never seemed more rigid than in metallurgy; yet the succession of forms tends to be replaced by the form of a continuous development, and the variability of matters tends to be replaced by the matter of a continuous variation. If metallurgy has an essential relation with music, it is by virtue not only of the sounds of the forge but also of the tendency within both arts to bring into its own, beyond separate forms, a continuous development of form, and beyond variable matters, a continuous variation of matter: a widened chromaticism sustains both music and metallurgy; the musical smith was the first 'transformer'.[32]

Blacksmithing concerns the increasing material *consistency* of metal itself, and has little to do with human intent or action. What holds matter together in these newly intensive states of consistency is, rather, a kind of syncopated attunement amongst interacting material forces, or what Deleuze and Guattari term a 'widened chromaticism,' as generated by audio synthesizers with multiple interacting oscillators. These intensive encounters make evident the lively flow of matter which is always present in the world, but typically hidden from perception by our tendency to focus only on static forms. What we tend to perceive within craft as the conservative repetition of the self-same is really the rhythm of matter in flux. Or, put differently, what repeats within craft is the vibrant potentiality of material change.

The same liveliness of co-construction Adorno sees in the finished artwork works all the way down. Or up, as it were. Either way, function is only one heterogeneous factor amongst many, and not an especially privileged one, even or especially in the negative. 'Interestedness' – that quality which for Adorno and Kant alike so fundamentally compromises the creative gesture – might be helpfully reconceived within craft practice as care. As de la Bellacasa notes in our epigraph, a materialist approach to care is not some *a priori* moralistic stance, but rather the necessarily collective sensuous attention to the haptic specifics of material encounter, precisely while resisting any such default categories or values. To approach craft as the collective craftwork of encounter requires engaging with the material world carefully and curiously, in full acknowledgement of the fact that practices are *never* individual or exclusively human, and cannot, therefore, be reduced to mere ideology.

---

32 Ibid.

Practices capable of resisting the status quo and opening new worlds are not given (or taken) in abstract criteria like autonomy, because they are not dreamt up and then perfunctorily executed by some thinking subject, alienated or otherwise. They are, rather, struggled for, and their questions and problems emerge only in the lived contingency of every encounter. We live today, not only at the threshold event of calamitous ecological destruction, but also, as Stengers phrases it, 'in a cemetery of already destroyed practices'. Rather than thinking the verb *to craft* in terms of the relative autonomy of critical free play, unconstrained by functionality and tradition, we need to fight for divergent practices of resistance, the factors of which are never singular or given abstractly in advance.

Yuka Oyama: *Piano*, 2016. From the series *Encapsulation Suits*.
Wearable sculpture made from black polyethylene. Photo: Attila Hartwig

From a System of Objects to Speculative Realism

André Gali

Artifacts can sometimes grow beyond their intended function. Some objects can demand from us a different set of rules in order to handle them. In some way or another, they take on a form of life within our minds. I thought, if commodities could evoke these various types of emotionality in us and construct fictions, then let them also become agents that help enhance our ability to imagine and dream.
– Yuka Oyama, 2017 [1]

Objects have biographies and ontologies, they come into being at some point in time and live lives of a certain length: maybe one second or 5,000 years. Through their existence, objects take part in shaping the world both physically and emotionally. For makers, creating and shaping objects to be used and/or experienced is the raison-d'étre. The objects may 'grow beyond their intended function', as Yuka Oyama describes it in the above quote.

Take a domestic object like a ceramic bowl – say one made from stoneware and raku fired in Japan in the Taishō period (1912–1926). Maybe it was fired in Tokyo in 1916 by Bernhard Leach and later brought to the UK where at some point it ended up in a museum collection. For this bowl to come into being at that specific time and place, many conditions had to be in place. Leach had to be in Japan (which he was), which in turn meant that he had to travel by boat from the UK at some point before the firing took place. And for that to happen, a boat needed to exist, and so forth. In addition to the many preconditions enabling Leach to be in Japan at that exact moment, there were other preconditions enabling the clay to exist: for starters, years of

---

1   Yuko Oyama, *The Stubborn Life of Objects*, Reflection on an artistic project 2012–2017, Oslo National Academy of the Arts, Department of Art and Craft, The Norwegian Artistic Research Fellowship Programme, Oslo (2017), 11.

geological processes in advance of the clay's excavation. For the firing to take place, there had already to be a forest to supply wood for the kiln. And so on.

Therefore: In order for the ceramic bowl we imagine here to come into existence, a number of events had to take place. And after the bowl was fired, perhaps it functioned as a soup bowl for many years. And for that to happen, a whole lot of other things had to be in place: a kitchen of sorts, a stove, a place to eat (table, chairs, floor), someone who knew how to make soup and, of course, the ingredients. And, if we pretend that the bowl ended up in a museum (which is likely), now it serves the more aesthetic function of providing sensory pleasure for lovers of ceramics. In some ways, it is dormant in the 'retirement home' that is the museum. But even for this to happen, a number of events would need to have taken place: first of all, the establishing of a museum with a collection, then a museum curator who chose this bowl to be exhibited, then the exhibition design, the plinth, etc.

We have thus established that this particular bowl has shaped the world in many ways that have unforeseen and unimaginable consequences, but that it also, over time, has been shaped by forces and other objects, some of which are human, others non-human. Furthermore, even though it may seem like the bowl, now in its museum condition, makes no fuss, it still effects the world and the objects around it. It is continuously shaped by the variety of forces and the objects with which it relates.

Clearly then, to set an object in motion in the world is a risky affair; you cannot control how it will be used, misused, abused, understood, misunderstood or handled, or what consequences may arise, be they historical, political, ecological, physical and so on. When an object is out in the world, it lives its own life, is defined by its own agency, the context in which it is situated and by the desires and agencies of other objects (human or non-human). Negotiations are constantly taking place between objects; they enter into relationships and networks, and they are involved in constant processes of becoming.

A critique of Kant
Contrary to what we have learned from the philosophy of Immanuel Kant (1724–1804) and what is often referred to as Kant's Copernican Revolution (rather than assuming that knowledge is shaped by reality

itself, it is our faculty of judgment that determines what reality is for us),[2] there are convincing theories that all objects (human or non-human) have an ontology, regardless of the human psyche or presence (which is the premise of Kant's experience with the world).[3] In fact, Kant's legacy is that we humans perceive there to be an unbridgeable gulf between, on one side, the world, reality or *the thing,* and on the other side, the human mind.[4] This I will refer to as *Kant's great divide*: with it comes the dualisms between subject and object, culture and nature, philosophy (reflection, interpretation) and science (physical laws), and so on. The trajectory that began with Kant's *Critiques*[5] has been pushed to the extreme limit in the hyper-reality of Postmodernism, for instance in the writings of Jean Baudrillard (1929–2007),[6] who describes simulacra and simulation as a total frenzy of images and abstractions that make humans into atoms circling in space, unattached to any reality, relationships or responsibility.

In this essay I discuss *what comes next* – after the erasure of reality, or after its marginalization, and how that relates to crafts. I look into what Jean Baudrillard, Bruno Latour (b. 1947) and Graham Harman (b. 1968) think about objects. Baudrillard, even though he in many

---

2   In the preface to the second edition of the *Critique of Pure Reason* (published in 1787; a heavy revision of the first edition of 1781), Immanuel Kant drew a parallel between the 'Copernican revolution' (when Nicolaus Copernicus showed that the earth is not the centre of the universe) and the epistemology of his new transcendental philosophy.

3   In Kant's work we find discussions of the autonomous object – or *thing-in-itself* – that exists outside the human perception, but Kant was unclear on the status of the object, and a result was that traditions of interpreting Kant's aesthetics in the 19th century related to the object only as the thing-for-me. This is the interpretation I base my critique of Kant on in this essay.

4   Dualism is of course much older than Kant. A certain branch of dualism is ascribed to Descartes, and this I will discuss a bit later on. Suffice it to say that through his writings, the concept of dualism was reinforced and became influential for the dominant philosophical thinking in modern Europe.

5   'The fundamental idea of Kant's "critical philosophy" – especially in his three Critiques: the *Critique of Pure Reason* (1781, 1787), the *Critique of Practical Reason* (1788), and the *Critique of the Power of Judgment* (1790) – is human autonomy.' Quoted from https://plato.stanford.edu/entries/kant/ (accessed on 15 November 2017).

6   See for instance Jean Baudrillard, *Simulations*, Semiotext(e) (Foreign Agent Series, 1983).

ways celebrates the erasure of reality, also points to how relationships between objects define the objects. This, in my view, can be seen as a starting point for discussing Latour's actor-network-theory, which defines objects by their attendant relationships. This theory seems to kick-start a return of reality, for lurking in the shadows of sociology, philosophy, ecology and art theory, reality once more grows strong. A new generation of philosophers is looking into this from a perspective called *Speculative Realism*.[7] Harman, being the most notable of these thinkers, has rewritten key ideas developed by the philosopher Martin Heidegger (1889–1976). Harman calls objects in the world (human and non-human) *tool-beings*, and describes his brand of Speculative Realism as *Object-Oriented Philosophy* (or ontology).[8] My point of view in this essay, at least to some extent, is that Postmodernism, as represented by Baudrillard,[9] emphasizes modern ideas put forth by Kant, but also paves the way for the New Realism in Latour's Actor-Network-Theory, which in turn leads to Harman's Object-Oriented Philosophy.[10]

Before exploring the ideas of the thinkers I have mentioned, and before giving supporting arguments for my claims, I want to say something about crafts – after all, this is precisely why I explore the ideas of these thinkers.

---

7   'Since its first appearance at a London colloquium in 2007, the speculative realism movement has taken continental philosophy by storm. Opposing the formerly ubiquitous modern dogma that philosophy can speak only of the human-world relation rather than the world itself, speculative realism defends the autonomy of the world from human access, but in a spirit of imaginative audacity.' Quote from https://edinburghuniversitypress.com/series-speculative-realism.html (accessed 15 November 2017)

8   You can get a pretty good idea of Graham Harman's intellectual journey from a devoted Heideggerian philosopher to an object-oriented ontologist in the book Graham Harman, *Toward Speculative Realism – Essays and Lectures* (Winchester: Zero Books, 2010).

9   I do not think Baudrillard himself ever used the term post-modern to describe his position, but I feel it is safe to do so in light of his basis in critical theory, Marxism and Structuralism.

10 Harman often uses the term 'Object-Oriented Philosophy' when referring to his branch of philosophy, but he uses the terms 'philosophy' and 'ontology' as basically the same thing. Ontology is usually understood as philosophy engaged in questions about the nature of being. To Harman, all philosophy concerns these kinds of questions.

Don't make art

In his text *Replacing the Myth of Modernism*,[11] the American studio jeweller and writer Bruce Metcalf warns craftspeople against trying to make works of art. 'Assimilation into art is deadly to craft, and should be avoided', he writes, and goes on to conclude that 'craft constitutes a different class of objects and also springs from a different set of values and a separate historical consciousness'. What interests me in this text is not only how Metcalf describes craft objects as different from art objects, but also that he makes it possible to see that craft objects may benefit from a being read in a way that differs from Kant's concept of the autonomous work of art.[12] But before going further, what does Metcalf mean by 'a separate historical consciousness'?

While modernist critics writing in the shadow of Kant (e.g., Theodor Adorno or Clement Greenberg) emphasize the autonomy of the object as the quality that secures its cultural value, craft objects seem to suffer when read in this manner. The way I understand Metcalf's definition, works of craft are not hermetic and autonomous objects; rather, they have four simultaneous identities or definitions:

> ... craft is usually made substantially by hand. ... craft is medium-specific: it is always identified with a material and the technologies invented to manipulate it. ... craft is defined by use ... craft is also defined by its past.[13]

This seems like an apt set of definitions to me, but the one that I think is most important in the present context concerns their *use*. On one hand, crafted objects relate to designed objects that are mass-produced, and on the other hand, to modern art. Yet as Metcalf points out, design and modern art have particular histories, theories and raison-d'être that

---

11   Bruce Metcalf, 'Replacing the Myth of Modernism', *American Craft*, vol. 53, no. 1 (February/March 1993). Also available at: http://www.brucemetcalf.com/pages/essays/replacing_myth.html (accessed 2 November 2017).

12   With a grounding in Kant's aesthetics, the concept of the autonomous work of art has become defining for Western modern and contemporary art. In short, the idea is that the work of art should be presented and experienced as transcending everyday life, and be perceived through a gaze that is free from desire. The work should be appreciated on its own terms, not in relation to terms applied by a viewer.

13   Metcalf, 'Replacing the Myth of Modernism'.

differ from the history, theory and purpose of the crafts. In my view, the aspect of *use* makes it patently clear that a work of craft is a social product that invites a user to get involved with it in a way that differs from the ways in which objects of art or design are used. We could, in fact, say that works of craft embody social engagement.[14] This is a quality they share with designed objects, even though they are not situated in the same context of production, industry, distribution and consumption. On the other hand, crafted objects also embody a conceptualization of reality or everyday life, just as might be the case for a work of art. But through the concept of *use* – as both actual engagement with the object or engagement with the idea of use – my proposition is that works of craft are both *relational* as well as *autonomous* objects.

In the following, I will not offer a new definition of craft. I try instead to offer a brief reading of objects that emphasizes their relation to a user or public and the understanding of objects in society at large. I couch my reading in a context that extends from French sociologist Jean Baudrillard's critique of Post-War Western culture's expanding consumer society, to the Speculative Realism of the American philosopher Graham Harman. The French sociologist Bruno Latour can be seen as a 'bridge' between French Postmodern thinking and the new orientation towards reality that we have experienced in recent years. He provides interesting perspectives on the relationship between human and non-human objects, or actors as he calls them. Latour has also influenced Harman, so much so that Harman wrote a book about him. This is why I read Latour in relation to Harman within the context of this text. That being said, Latour also relates to issues that were seen as important to the French thinkers of his generation, and Harman in turn differentiates himself from Latour on some key issues. When presenting the theories of Baudrillard, Latour and Harman, I will also present analyses of selected works by the craft artists Yuka Oyama (b. 1974), Elin Hedberg (b. 1988) and Heidi Børgan (b. 1970), as a way of 'fleshing out' my thoughts.

---

14 In this analysis, I am limiting the concept of design objects to manufactured objects for everyday use. I do not take into account other types of design such as web design or service design.

A system of objects

The quote with which this essay starts is from Yuko Oyama's written reflection on *The Stubborn Life of Objects*, her artistic research project at Oslo National Academy of Arts.[15] Oyama set out to investigate the relationship between herself and five domestic objects – a bag of flour, a handbag, a headdress, a key and a piano – which she chose due to the emotional value they held for her. These objects were then the basis for five wearable sculptures which Oyama called 'encapsulation suits'. They are made from black Polyethylene (PE) sponge – a material used to isolate heat and sound.[16] Considering her background in art jewellery (Oyama studied under the renowned jewellery artist and professor Otto Künzli in Munich) and her interest in the relationships that arise between wearers and jewellery as well as jewellery and the public, it does not seem surprising that Oyama decided to investigate these domestic objects with methods common to performance art. In this context, the traditional subject-object relationship is altered and the objects gain an additional dimension. In fact, the encapsulation suits succeed in showing how objects can be agents that define a given situation and shape human movement. Oyama describes an object as a co-actor in this relationship, but one could also say that the human being is, to some extent, the prop for the object-actor.

For French sociologist and philosopher Jean Baudrillard – possibly mostly known for introducing the concepts of 'simulacra' and 'hyper reality' into contemporary thinking[17] – objects in consumer culture enter into the same sort of relationships with people as Oyama describes in her project; the difference, however, is that Baudrillard sees the objects as controlling the individual primarily in their capacity as signs. Baudrillard's initial intention was to do a neo-Marxist critique

15 Yuka Oyama was a research fellow at the Art and Craft Department, Oslo National Academy of the Arts, during 2012–2017. More information on Yuka Oyama and this project are available at https://www.yukaoyama.com (accessed 15 November 2017).

16 Yuko Oyama, *The Stubborn Life of Objects*, 21.

17 In 1983 Jean Baudrillard gained international recognition through the booklet *Simulations*, Semiotext(e) (Foreign Agent Series). Suggested reading for more information on this book – *André Gali: This summer I am re-reading… Jean Baudrillard's Simulations* (Art Jewelry Forum): https://artjewelryforum.org/articles-series/this-summer-i-am-re-reading%E2%80%A6 (accessed 15 November 2017).

of consumer society inspired by the Situationist Internationale and Guy Debord, especially his book *The Society of the Spectacle*.[18] Debord's idea was that human lives are merely fiction staged by media, fashion, design and art, but Baudrillard left this position and eventually developed an understanding of contemporary (Western) capitalist society as being defined by signs and systems of signs, or codes and matrixes.[19] According to Baudrillard, there is no such thing as reality, only simulacra; the copy and the original, the artificial and the real, have merged and are impossible to distinguish from each other.[20]

A book by Baudrillard that has gained increased attention from makers and artists lately, among others from Yuka Oyama,[21] is the first book he published in France in 1968. It was translated into English in 1996 under the title *The System of Objects*.[22] Here we find Baudrillard's first attempt to analyse and develop a language for discussing the mass-production of everyday objects in an expanding consumer society. He pays a lot of attention to domestic objects and asks two key questions: 'What mental structures are interwoven with – and contradict – their [everyday objects] functional structures?' 'What cultural, infracultural or transcultural system underpins their directly experienced everydayness?'[23] Obviously, the mass production and distribution of consumer objects are not neutral gestures of making functional and/or decorative objects available for people at reasonable prices; to the contrary, they serve to produce and distribute signifiers of identity (class, culture, taste, etc.), as a way of defining where people belong in a cultural and economic hierarchy in (a mobile) society.[24] Baudrillard held this view at the time he wrote *The System of Objects* because, he said, in (Western capitalist) society, 'there are two entangled social orders – *the*

---

18 Guy Debord, *The Society of the Spectacle* (New York: ZoneBooks, 1994, original in French 1967).

19 In fact, Jean Baudrillard's texts were the inspiration for the science fiction movies *The Matrix Trilogy* (1999–2003, written and directed by the Wachowskis).

20 Jean Baudrillard, *Simulations*, Semiotext(e) (Foreign Agent Series, 1993).

21 Oyama refers to the book in her thesis.

22 Jean Baudrillard, *The System of Objects* (London: Verso, 2005, original in French 1968).

23 Ibid., 2.

24 This is also the subject of Baudrillard's second book, *The Consumer Society – Myths and Structures* (London: Sage, 1998, original in French 1970).

order of production London: Verso, 2005 *and the order of consumption'.*[25] And in the order of consumption, objects function primarily as social signs. Some years later he abandoned the idea of an order of production and the idea that media and consumer products are representations of a (Marxist) material reality. He began instead to explore the idea that there are now only representations, or simulacra – there is nothing real, as mentioned above. What in fact signifies objects in *The System of Objects*, and what matters to us here, is the idea that objects lose their autonomy as objects and gain their value as part of various sign-systems, similar to how a language is structured by words that primarily gain meaning when they enter into relationships with other words in sentences or other language structures.

After the orgy of modernity

Baudrillard's analysis of contemporary society has been of great benefit to me personally, not least when I was doing my master thesis on Andy Warhol's pop persona.[26] But in the context of what we discuss here, I think it is safe to say that Baudrillard has only pushed the idea of the divide between objects and subjects to its final conclusion. He does not see objects as real things; they only exist for him as signs, as representations of things that lack real presence. Objects are copies but not based on anything original. In defining objects as part of a system, the objects gain their characteristics from the relationships in which they appear. This is interesting in light of Bruno Latour and the actor-network-theory, as we will soon see.

In many ways Baudrillard takes the full consequence of Kant's great divide. But his position reminds us even more of another great grandfather of modern philosophy, the French philosopher and mathematician René Descartes (1596–1650), who reduced the whole of reality to human perception when he reached the conclusion that 'I think, therefore I am'.[27] In his path towards this conclusion, Descartes doubted everything that existed – what he believed to be real could, he feared,

---

25 Ibid., 8.

26 André Gali, *Andy Warhol Superstar: On the Artist Myth, Media and Mechanical Theatricality*, thesis, University of Oslo, Norway, 2005. (The thesis is in Norwegian.)

27 René Descartes reached this conclusion in the book that was published in French in 1637 and translated as *Discourse on Method*.

actually be a dream or a fantasy imposed upon him by the devil. What he could not doubt was the fact that he was thinking – for how could he doubt anything if he did not think? It was impossible for Descartes to understand how the physical world and the mental world could communicate with each other, except with help from God. Only then did he find it possible to re-connect with reality. Like Descartes, Baudrillard reaches the same desolate situation in his thinking. What he believes to be true and factual is merely a mirage – a system of signs disguised as objects. But for Baudrillard it is not the devil who lures the human mind into a dream or fantasy; no, the images of modern media are the culprits – the (over)production of representations and copies, representations of representations, copies of copies, codes and matrixes – and since there is no God (after Nietzsche 'killed him') there is no way back to reality. Baudrillard wrote several of his theories before the Internet was invented, but in many ways he foresaw the simulacra of the always-online computer: in so many ways admirable, but also a sort of endgame for Cartesian and Kantian thinking.

In a fin-de-millennium spirit, Baudrillard's book *The Transparency of Evil* (French version 1990) describes modernity as an endless orgy – a liberation of politics, sex, art and models of representation – and he asks: '*What do we do after the orgy?*'[28]

This question seems to suggest that Baudrillard has a misanthropic view of contemporary society, but in a later interview, he reveals that after the orgy there is *hope*:

> What do we do after the orgy of modernity? Is simulation all we have left? /... / this expression – 'after the orgy' – comes from a story full of hope: it is the story of a man who whispers into the ear of a woman during an orgy, 'What are you doing after the orgy?' There is always the hope of a new seduction.[29]

Readjusting reality

When encountering Elin Hedberg's metal and wooden works, we as viewers are 'seduced' into engaging physically with the objects. For the exhibition *Readjustment* (2015), she built a shelf structure in the

28 Jean Baudrillard, *The Transparency of Evil: Essays on Extreme Phenomena* (London: Verso, 1993), 3.

29 Jean Baudrillard, *The Conspiracy of Art: Manifestos, Interviews, Essays,* ed. Sylvère Lotringer (New York: Semiotext(e)/MIT Press, 2005), 98–110.

middle of a small room and placed various wooden and metal objects on the shelves.[30] The works were inviting, shaped as vessels or vases, but with no actual function. They seemed to want to be lifted and held as much as looked at. Both the shelving and the objects seemed familiar and strange at the same time; the presentation and the domestic shapes triggered a desire to want to touch the objects, to sense their weight and feel their surface qualities. When experiencing *Readjustment*, our physical engagement was *as* important as viewing the objects, maybe even more so. Oftentimes we were surprised: what appeared to be a vase would not have an opening, what seemed light in weight would in fact be heavy. Structures in the wood and metal also underscored the sensory experience. It could be said about Hedberg's exhibition that she engaged with the vase as a leitmotif, but it was more than that: Hedberg did not create the sculptures primarily in order to depict the vase as an art historical subject. Her works in the exhibition focused more on the user and the user's experience of being in direct contact with the works.

Thinking about Hedberg's works in the context of art theory, I am reminded of the French curator and theorist Nicolas Bourriaud and his concepts of *relational art* and *relational aesthetics*.[31] Put simply, relational art focuses on human relationships and their social contexts, on establishing relationships more than on making works of art in a traditional sense (as autonomous works to be viewed from a distance). Relational aesthetics points to a way of judging artworks based on the inter-human relations they represent, produce or prompt. However, Hedberg's art draws as much on the specific tradition of metalworking (silversmithing and hollowware) and the history of the beholder, not to mention the relationship established by objects (human and non-human) when a function comes into play, as on Bourriaud's key concepts. Her works are not exactly functional, but they do relate to shapes and materials we recognize from functional objects. They awaken something in our body and in our hands, something not grounded primarily

---

30 Early works by Elin Hedberg can be found at her website, among them, the exhibition *Readjustment* (2015), which was her master's degree show that same year. It was on account of *Readjustment* that she received the 'Master Student Award' from the Norwegian Association for Arts and Crafts. http://elinhedberg.se (accessed 20 November 2017).

31 Nicolas Bourriaud, *Relational Aesthetics* (Dijon: Les Presses du Reel, 2002).

Elin Hedberg: *Readjustment*, 2015. MDF, wood, copper, cast iron.
Photos: Henrik Sörensen

in our intellect. In fact, the way Hedberg goes about it differs greatly from the approach by contemporary art-theory star Bourriaud, who still in some respects – even though challenging the concept of autonomous art – thinks within the tradition of Kant. Bourriaud comes to relationality in the wake of Kant, seemingly not realizing that relationships always have been part of aesthetic experience, even if not so much in the segment of modern and contemporary art.

Actor-network-theory

These works of Hedberg are not autonomous objects or representations in a Kantian sense, but must be understood in a materialistic way, as evoking immediate reactions located in the body of the viewer. Hedberg's works are all about a material experience, thus challenging the Kantian hierarchy between subject and object. In fact, they make me think of the actor-network-theory conceptualized by French sociologist Bruno Latour.[32]

Opposing the modernist philosophy of Kant and the relativist philosophy of his contemporary countrymen,[33] Latour says that reality consists of *actors* or *actants*. In this reality, non-human objects have ontological status equal to that of human objects. In other words, Latour theorizes the erasure of the divide between humans and the world, and the supposed hierarchy between the human subject and the object. His book *Reassembling the Social – An Introduction to Actor-Network-Theory* (2005) discusses the role of objects:

> Much like sex during the Victorian period, objects are nowhere to be said and everywhere to be felt. They exist, naturally, but they are never given a thought, a social thought. Like humble servants, they live on the margins of the social doing most of the work but never allowed to be represented as such.[34]

---

32 There are several authors writing on actor-network-theory, of which Michel Callon, Bruno Latour and John Law are the most known. In this paragraph I build my arguments on Bruno Latour, most notably his book *Reassembling the Social – An Introduction to Actor-Network-Theory* (Oxford: Oxford University Press, 2005), and Graham Harman, *Prince of Networks: Bruno Latour and Metaphysics* (Melbourne: re.press, 2009).

33 'French philosophy', writes Graham Harman, in his book *Prince of Networks*, 'was merely a collective nickname in the Anglophone mind for Michel Foucault and Jacques Derrida' (p. 12).

34 Bruno Latour, *Reassembling the Social,* 73.

Objects set us in motion, activate or passivate us at will and define our movements and bodily actions. This they do through their assembled qualities, be they functional, material, spatial, moral and so forth. They instruct other object (in this case people) to act in a certain way. It is worth holding this in mind while reflecting on Hedberg's works, for they highlight the relationship between people and objects. The social life of her objects comes to the fore, and we as viewers become bodily aware of their qualities.

As I mentioned in the introduction, using an imaginary bowl as my example, objects don't just come out of nowhere – in Latourian terminology, they belong to ongoing *networks of events*. As such, the event of a work by Hedberg entering into a relationship with a human actor is preceded by many events, of which the making and exhibiting of the work obviously is included. Where, when and how a work is presented is important to our analysis, because if these aspects were not in place, we as human actors would engage with the work under different circumstances, or not at all. If we were to trace some of the actors who have entered into the networks that made this event come into being, we could start with the work of art and trace it back through the process of making – the work carries, in this respect, a story of its 'birth' and 'life' – and all the things that must be in place for this specific object to come into being. Obviously, material, tools, workshop, skills and a maker must be in place, but for all the various preconditioning actors, there are any number of other actors, events and networks that are engaged. The specific material comes from somewhere, the tools have been made by someone, the workshop was built, and so forth. It would be impossible to trace all these networks, but they are all crucial for the work's existence. The same is true for the human actors who view the work: we also belong to endless networks of human and non-human actors. It therefore seems warranted to say that the actor-network-theory not only challenges the notion of the autonomous object, it challenges the romantic notion of the genius artist (which still is very much alive today) and the post-Kantian idea of the human being as hierarchically superior to non-human actors. Latour's idea of the human actor as on the same footing as any other objects (human or non-human, natural or artificial) is fully *post-human*, a term often used about object-oriented ontology, which we will turn to shortly. But before doing so, let's look at a case of how 'autonomous objects' exist in a network.

Networks and autonomous objects

For Heidi Bjørgan, exhibitions are composed of relationships between objects as much as by objects as autonomous beings or works of art. Bjørgan has established herself as both a noteworthy ceramist and a curator. By blending her artistic practice with curating, she erases the opposition between production (making) and distribution (showing). Most notably, when she made the exhibition *The Story of an Affair* at Nordenfjeldske Kunstindustrimuseum in 2016 – an exhibition in which she as maker and curator entered into dialogue with the museum's collection – the blurring between her own works, the works of the collection and the exhibition design rendered the exhibition itself as the object of experience.[35] Through the numerous relations established in this exhibition – between the different objects, between contemporary objects and historical objects, and between the objects and their surroundings (the immediate space, but also the museum and the town of Trondheim where the museum is located) – the exhibition became a multi-layered and almost holistic experience. In her making and curating, Bjørgan also explores and comments on traditions of displaying works of craft in exhibitions. Drawing on ideas from film and scenography, she turns the objects into actors in both a theatrical sense and in a Latourian sense as discussed above. Several interesting networks can be traced from this exhibition. One readily traceable connection is to Nordenfjeldske Kunstindustrimuseum: as a specific object, physically, as a building of a certain size and made from certain materials, and as a carrier of many stories, for instance, those telling about discursive art exhibitions from which the art scene in Trondheim may have benefitted, and all the events leading to the specific works that have been acquired for the museum's collection. At some point in time, the history of the museum is entangled with the biography of the curator-maker Heidi Børgan. This may even be one reason why Bjørgan decided to become a maker and a curator. As we have seen, all objects serve actively in events that shape the world, and these networks of events are tremendous. Some events may be brief encounters while other may extend across generations, and that

---

35 For more information on Heidi Bjørgan's exhibition in Trondheim, see Jorunn Veiteberg, 'A Baroque Fairytale of an Exhibition', at *NorwegianCrafts.no*: http://www.norwegiancrafts.no/articles/a-baroque-fairytale-of-an-exhibition (accessed 30 November 2017).

which constitutes an object – or actor, which is Latour's preferred term – are the relations in which it participates. Some encounters between Bjørgan and Nordenfjeldske Kunstindustrimuseum were reassembled and reactivated in the exhibition, as she returned to objects that mean a lot to her and inspired her in her youth.

As I mention in the introduction, the philosopher Graham Harman is very fond of Latour and has related his own critique of philosophers such as Kant and Heidegger to Latour's actor-network-theory. In *The Prince of Networks – Bruno Latour and Metaphysics,*[36] Harman analyses what he sees as Latour's contribution to philosophy. In fact, he characterizes Latour as 'a pioneer of object-oriented philosophy'.[37] In Harman's terminology, this is a branch of philosophy that treats objects as deserving the same sort of philosophical investigation as do human beings. As the attentive reader may have noticed, we have now moved away from sociology – Baudrillard and Latour both have backgrounds in sociology – to philosophy. Harman studies Latour's writings and discusses what kind of philosophy they present to readers. He concludes that Latour's philosophy belongs to metaphysics because it deals with fundamental questions about being, existence and reality. Latour's world, as we have seen, is made up of actors and actants:

> Atoms and molecules are actants, as are children, raindrops, bullet trains, politicians, and numerals. All entities are on exactly the same ontological footing.[38]

But, says Harman (after having gone thoroughly through Latour's development of key concepts in the actor-network-theory), 'we find little discussion of relations between inanimate entities when people are nowhere on the scene'.[39] Harman concludes, first, that Latour ultimately discusses objects from the perspective of the relation to or the influence they have on a human actor, and, second, that for Latour, objects are defined by relationships more than by having an autonomous reality. This latter point is crucial to Harman's critique of Latour.

---

36 Graham Harman, *Prince of Networks.*

37 Ibid., 151.

38 Ibid., 14.

39 Ibid., 158.

Heidi Bjørgan: *Story of an Affair*. 2016. Installation view and details from the exhibition. Photo: Thor Brødreskrift/Nordenfjeldske Kunstindustrimuseum, Trondheim

Object-oriented ontology

In the book *The Speculative Turn: Continental Materialism and Realism*,[40] which Harman has co-edited, you can read that 'the new breed of thinker is turning once more toward reality itself'. While these thinkers may have very different approaches, one common trait is that they 'have begun speculating once more about the nature of reality independently of thought and of humanity more generally'.[41] What the speculative realists turn away from are thinkers like Jean Baudrillard, mentioned above, and other French philosophers such as Michel Foucault and Jacques Derrida. While their textual and social critique has been valuable, there is a need to go beyond the human perspective and social structure in order to address reality. And as an alternative method for doing critical analysis, the new thinkers offer the methodology of speculation, which they describe as a kind of *pre-critical* approach.[42] This is understood as the kind of philosophical thought that existed before Kant's Critiques – maybe we could explain it as a way of thinking that is more closely associated with a pre-modern way of thinking than that of Derrida, Foucault and Baudrillard. The dualism (subject-object, culture-nature, etc.) of modern philosophy is seen as a 'detour philosophy', and it is in this sense that Latour has claimed that *we have never been modern*.[43]

For Harman, Latour is an important thinker in this turn towards reality, but Harman looks differently at what objects are. In one of his most substantial books, *Tool-Being: Heidegger and the Metaphysics of Objects*,[44] he defines objects through *use*. He explains that objects – *tool-beings* as he calls them – are constantly being used, even when we are unaware of it. This he derives from Heidegger's tool-analysis

40 Levi Bryant, Nick Srnicek and Graham Harman, *The Speculative Turn: Continental Materialism and Realism* (Melbourne: re.press, 2011).

41 Ibid., 3.

42 Ibid.

43 Bruno Latour, *We Have Never Been Modern* (Chicago: Harvard University Press, 1993). In Latours's book, he explores how a certain concept of dualism, which conceives of the humanities and science as fully autonomous fields and as antithetical to each other, has been defining for the concept of modernity. He states that this dualism – and thus the fundament of modernism – is a misconception of reality.

44 Graham Harman, *Tool-Being, Heidegger and the Metaphysics of Objects* (Chicago: Open Court, 2002).

in *Being and Time*.[45] I don't have the space to elaborate on Heidegger's view on tools here; suffice it to say that according to Heidegger, we humans use tools in a kind of automatic way, unless they break. When that happens, we become conscious of their existence, and our own. In this way, tools exist *for* humans.

Harman agrees with this view of tools, but he differs from Heidegger when he claims that human objects are not the only ones to use inanimate or non-human objects. Such objects also use each other, and they use humans. All objects are *tool-beings* that constantly use each other, he says, and they are therefore similar to Latour's actors in the way they enter into relationships and networks with each other. But Harman also points out that objects have a sort of substance and autonomy. Objects are agents with a biography, ontology and relationships to other objects – their existence is defined by their *tool-being* – they are *tools* (in the Heideggerian sense) and *beings* or autonomous entities of sorts.

In Harman's view, objects shape each other regardless of any human presence; they have relationships with each other that are inaccessible to humans. We can only speculate or imagine these relationships. Take for instance the relation between a vase and the plinth it rests upon in Bjørgan's exhibition, between the plinth and the floor at Nordenfjeldske Kunstindustrimuseum, between the nails that hold the plinth together, and so forth. These relationships are most real, but we humans have no direct access to them. Still, they play roles in shaping the world.

Conclusion

The three artists – or makers of contemporary crafts – whom I have discussed here all manifest in various ways the social life of objects. I chose them because their artistic practices help elucidate the thoughts presented by Baudrillard, Latour and Harman.

In the case of Yuka Oyama, her objects become co-actors on a stage where psychodrama is played out. With her primary media of performance and filmed performance, the agency of objects is set in motion through a psychological framing. Relationships between actors seem

---

45 Martin Heidgegger, *Being and Time* (Albany, NY: State University of New York, original in German, 1927).

to fluctuate, yet at the same time, the objects represent a sort of stability for Oyama (as she explains in her thesis). The objects she chooses to enlarge and to 'devour' the human actors are highly consequential for her project. But the objects exceed her intentions and live lives of their own. Through use, they become animated and thus shed light on their dual meaning: they are actors in their own right, but also carriers of Oyama's projected intentions.

In the case of Elin Hedberg, her objects are seemingly autonomous works of art meant to be viewed from a distance, but when entering the exhibition space, we as viewers are drawn to them (as is often the case for many people in art museums – only we have been taught not to touch the works). The objects reach out to us through their material, form and appearance. Resembling functional objects with vessel shapes, the objects – be they wood or metal – invite us to enter into a particular relationship. This is relational art that does not limit itself to establishing relationships between human actors – as Bourriaud's definition of relational aesthetics indicates – for it establishes relationships between all actors (in a Latourian sense), whether human or not. As actors, we are invited to reflect on the networks that we and the work of art are engaging in, and we enter into a relationship with the work both physically and emotionally.

In the case of Heidi Bjørgan, the objects are set in an environment that emphasizes the relationships established between the objects themselves. At the same time as this is happening, the objects, which demand an autonomous space, also establish numerous networks linking them to historical events, people, institutions, geological events, and so forth. We can use Bjørgan's exhibition as a metaphor: the works enter into relationships with each other, both physically and emotionally, but they also have their individual and autonomous space and agency. In our context, it may seem futile to speculate over the hidden life of these objects, the relations we cannot access, but it is still important to acknowledge the complexity of objects. This complexity extends beyond the maker's control and intention, and beyond mere materiality, function and concept. All objects shape the world we inhabit, and works of contemporary craft function as specific kinds of objects that embody and shape the material world as well as the emotional world of human objects.

What I have tried to argue for here by referring to Latour and Harman's understanding of objects is that what differentiates contemporary crafts from design and/or art is that crafts seek to engage the viewer bodily, with the object at hand, through use or the reference to use, but that they also engage with the history of the discipline and address the relationship between the human body, the object and the social sphere. Through addressing that relationship, a work of craft also engages in reflection and critical thinking about the social sphere. Put differently, crafts have the potential to offer a bodily experience of the relationship between the human actant, the non-human actant and the social context, as well as asking the viewer (in lieu of a better word) to engage critically and conceptually in the same relationship. As I stated at the beginning of this essay, my aim is not to offer a new definition of crafts – I am completely happy with Bruce Metcalf's definition (which is more detailed than presented here) – but I have dug into the aspect of use to see if it is possible to locate an even broader meaning of it if we add thoughts from Latour and Harman to the discussion. And as we have seen, the concept of *use* is essential to the way Harman understands the object or tool-being. The object is both a tool to be used, and an autonomous agent.

Unknown: *Picture – Shepheard Buss*, 1570–1600. Embroidered linen in silk, bobbin lace. In the collection of the Victoria and Albert Museum, London. © Victoria and Albert Museum, London.

Craft and the Allegorical Impulse

Glenn Adamson

Author's note

I had originally intended, when writing *Thinking Through Craft* (2007), to include a chapter on Allegory. The book addressed craft's marginalization within modernity, particularly in relation to fine art. My central argument was that Modern art defined itself, in part, through its dissociation from craft. I had arrived at this position through reading the work of Postcolonial and Feminist theorists. Much as study of the ethnographic Other has served to reinforce Eurocentric views of normalcy, or the feminine has been described negatively in such a way as to assert phallocentric authority, craft has been treated as a margin or 'horizon', incompatible with serious artwork. In developing this theme, I looked at a series of interrelated pairings – autonomous/supplemental, optical/material, institutional/pastoral, professional/amateur. Craft in each case is associated with the latter, unprivileged term. The book also has a fifth, central chapter on 'skill', the pivot around which the book was meant to turn, which marks the shift from the formal issues, addressed in the first two chapters, to issues of social context, taken up in the last two.

I had expected that the opposition between symbol and allegory would make another of these dialectical chapters. I didn't quite manage that, though, and ended up shelving the research. Now, ten years on and thanks to the invitation of this volume's editors, 'later' has arrived. So consider the following to be a long-delayed supplement to *Thinking Through Craft* – sort of like a DVD extra. My treatment of the theme of allegory is necessarily different from how I might have approached it in the 1990s, not least because of the tremendous shifts in craft practice, criticism and scholarship that have occurred since then. Understanding the power plays of Modern art seems less urgent today, when there are so many ongoing questions about craft's cultural and political efficacy; being able to theorize the enigmatic potency of craft, on its own terms, seems more important. Even so, I invite you to read this text as 'unfinished business' – which is, come to think of it, what the allegorical impulse is all about.

Unknown: *Cabinet*, c. 1650. Barniz de Pasto lacquer. Vice-royalty of Peru (Colombia). Given by Dr. Robert MacLeod Coupe and Heather Coupe in memory of their brother, Philip MacLeod Coupe. In the collection of the Victoria and Albert Museum, London. © Victoria and Albert Museum, London

In 1980 the American critic Craig Owens published an essay in two parts, entitled 'The Allegorical Impulse: A Theory of Postmodernism'. His goal was to recuperate allegory as a renewed foundation for art practice. The essay was widely influential in the ensuing decade, so much so that today it might be considered a dead letter, a document that had its day and then became irrelevant. Yet, central to his argument was the notion of repeated return. Owens asserted that the allegorical mode had been inimical to Modernism, 'proscribed territory', 'an aesthetic aberration, the antithesis of art'.[1] His intention was to reintroduce it, and at the same time, to reinvent it. Allegory was a particularly apt subject for such a manoeuvre, for as we will see, it can be understood metaphorically as a constantly renewable field of fragments, like an architectural ruin, ever ready for re-inhabitation. It is in this same spirit that we might profitably read Owens' text. Though quintessentially of its time, it also has much to offer us today.

One of the curious features of twentieth-century writings about allegory is the way that they disguise wild flashes of creativity under thick layers of scholarly apparatus – think of the writings of Jorge Luis Borges, for example. Owens' essay is no exception. In some passages, 'The Allegorical Impulse' comes across almost as a literature review: a lucid exposition of texts. At the centre of his account is Walter Benjamin's book *The Origin of German Tragic Drama* (*Ursprung des deutschen Trauerspiels*, 1927). But Owens' overall goal is more provocative than mere historiography. He does not so much define his key term as deploy it, somewhat elliptically, and without committing to a single simple usage. Allegory, he writes, is 'an attitude as well as a technique, a perception as well as a procedure'. That is pretty obscure, but then he continues: 'Let us say for the moment that allegory occurs whenever one text is doubled by another.' More precisely, it can be described as 'a single metaphor introduced in continuous series', which 'superinduces a vertical or paradigmatic reading of correspondences upon a horizontal or syntagmatic chain of events'. Allegory leaps across established disciplines and categories: 'the allegorical work is synthetic, it

---

1   Craig Owens, 'The Allegorical Impulse: Toward a Theory of Postmodernism', part one, *October,* vol 12 (Spring, 1980), 67–86: 67.

crosses aesthetic boundaries'. Emotionally, it is an elegiac mode, 'consistently attracted to the fragmentary, the imperfect, the incomplete'.[2]

Following this somewhat elusive theoretical exposition, Owens proceeds to apply the concept of allegory to a range of artists working in a range of styles: appropriationists like Sherrie Levine and Robert Longo; Robert Rauschenberg, for his thickly encoded 'combines', which can be read like rebuses; artists who engage in serial composition, like Carl Andre and Hanne Darboven; and Laurie Anderson, she of the shifting, beguiling and multiple voices. Over the course of the two parts of the essay, it becomes clear that what binds together these varied artists is more a philosophical stance than a specific methodology. Owens positions the 'allegorical impulse' as the core principle of Postmodernism. For him, the mode involves reading and re-scripting rather than creating anew, piling up fragments rather than seeking an integrated whole, and conceiving of works as being in endless series rather than as cases of definitive, closed form.

Owens was paving new ground in applying the concept of allegory to visual art, instead of leaving it in its traditional domain, literature. But he was by no means the only theorist who sought to revive allegory as part of the Postmodern turn. He was part of a generation of Post-Structuralists who, as Joel Black has written, believed that 'each reading of the "same" text, by different readers at different times, produces a different "object" which is never the same in any two readings'.[3] Critics inclined to be hostile to this sort of relativism attacked writers like Owens for 'elevating unintelligibility of relationship into [a] central aesthetic principle' – a typically impatient response to Postmodernist indeterminacy.[4] But such conservative views missed the sophistication of Owens' essay. He was certainly innovative, in that he found in allegory a poetic basis for Postmodern expression, quite different from the more overtly political conceptions of the term by the likes

---

2   Owens, 'The Allegorical Impulse', part one, 68, 72, 75, 70.

3   Joel D. Black, 'Allegory Unveiled', in *Poetics Today*, vol. 4, no. 1 (1983), 109–126: 112. Among Post-Structuralist literary critics, Paul de Man was particularly influential in implementing the concept of allegory as part of his radical destabilization of textual meaning. See Paul de Man, *Allegories of Reading* (New Haven: Yale University Press, 1979).

4   James Applewhite, 'Postmodern Allegory and the Denial of Nature', *The Kenyon Review*, vol. 11, no. 1 (Winter, 1989), 1–17: 5.

of Jean-François Lyotard, Fredric Jameson and Jürgen Habermas. Nonetheless, Owens was operating within a tradition of profound thought. As we will see, even as he showed the implications of allegory for then-nascent Postmodernism, his text also offered routes back into the pre-modern tradition, and forward to our own post-Postmodern moment. It is therefore worth retrieving 'The Allegorical Impulse' for present-day use. In this essay, I propose to do this, retracing the intellectual lineage of allegory, while simultaneously trying to render the idea more accessible and concrete.

In doing so, I will shift emphasis away from the type of works that Owens considered – broadly speaking, conceptual artworks that are metonymic in their structure – and instead ground my discussion within the history and theory of craft. I am sure that Owens himself would have found this a surprising move, for not a single one of the artists he discussed was oriented towards skilled workmanship; nor indeed was Postmodern practice generally.[5] Yet a consideration of craft, that much neglected term in so much theory, does seem consistent with the expansionist and metaphorical approach that he brought to the topic; his goal was to avoid rigid binaries, and instead explore structures of layering and simultaneity.[6] It seems entirely suitable to consider craft within such a permissive intellectual context. As it happens, there are also stray observations in Owens' text that indicate the specific suitability of allegorical thinking to arrive at a deeper understanding of crafted objects. Following these traces back into the literature, we can begin to take the measure of a powerful and untapped body of thought, which sheds its light (or perhaps it would be better to say, casts its shadow) on artisanal practice.

Allegory and symbol

In an effort to establish firmer purchase on the term allegory, it is helpful first to see it in relation to the term to which it is most frequently contrasted: symbol. The terminology here is slippery; authors vary in their handling of this important dichotomy, with Angus Fletcher,

5   On this point, see my essay 'Substance Abuse: The Postmodern Surface', in *Surface Tensions,* eds. Glenn Adamson and Victoria Kelley (Manchester: Manchester University Press, 2013).

6   I am indebted on this point to my colleague Ulrich Lehmann, whom I thank for his constructive reading of this essay in manuscript.

whom I will discuss at some length below, describing allegory as a 'symbolic mode'. And in any case, the whole point of allegory is to avoid stark dialectical thinking, so we should understand the relation here as one of difference rather than actual opposition. The basic distinction, however, is as follows. A 'symbol' is a unitary sign. It may stand in for a divine entity – as a cross stands for Christ, for example – though it can also be secular, as with a dove that represents peace. The crucial point is that a symbol stands in a one-to-one metaphorical relationship with its referent. Classically, the symbol has been understood to possess qualities of clarity, brevity, grace, radiance and beauty.

Allegory can be briefly defined, in contrast, as 'continuous metaphor'. If a symbol has a unified and potentially transcendent character, then allegory is an open-ended, often narrative mode, in which multiple images or emblems correlate to an external referent, which is itself multiple and complex. As Walter Benjamin beautifully put it, 'allegory provides the dark background against which the bright world of the symbol might stand out'.[7] It is by nature multivalent, offering numerous anchor-points that bind together two or more layers of meaning. To quote the literary theorist William Empson: 'The effect of allegory is to keep the two levels of being very distinct in your mind, though they interpenetrate each other in so many details.'[8]

Allegory dates back to ancient times, to texts such as Plato's *Republic*, with its famous parable of the cave. Well-known modern instances include Franz Kafka's *The Trial*, Albert Camus' *The Plague,* George Orwell's *Animal Farm*, and Margaret Atwood's *The Handmaid's Tale*, all of which employ fable-like stories that echo contemporary political and social situations. A good contemporary example is the stage musical *Hamilton*, which retells the biography of one of the founding fathers of the USA in such a way as to hold a mirror up to twenty-first-century, multicultural America. It is also worth noting that texts can also be read allegorically, that is, subjected to retrospective metaphorical readings, as when stories from the Old Testament are interpreted as prefigurations of the life of Christ.

---

7   Walter Benjamin, *The Origin of German Tragic Drama*
    [Ursprung des deutschen Trauerspiels], trans. John Osborne
    (New York: Verso, 1988, original in German 1928, 161.

8   William Empson, *Structure of Complex Words*
    (London: Chatto and Windus, 1951), 347.

While the opposition between symbol and allegory has its roots in Classical rhetoric, it was only in the Romantic era that it was codified, mainly in order to assert the precedence of the former. Samuel Taylor Coleridge and Thomas Carlyle, two prominent contributors to this development, seized on the symbol for its unity of form and content, the material and the metaphysical. They argued that symbols were the ideal (perhaps the only) means through which artistic imagination could body itself forth. Both men explicitly contrasted such 'true works of art' with allegories, which Carlyle dismissed as offering nothing but 'the Daub of Artifice'.[9] As Bainard Cowan has written, from this point onwards, allegory 'came to be seen as mere convention, inauthentic, not grounded in experience, cut off from being and concerned only with manipulating its repertoire of signs'.[10] This Romantic-era judgment cascaded down to the twentieth century, with the poet W. B. Yeats, for example, writing:

> A symbol is indeed the only possible expression of some invisible essence, a transparent lamp about a spiritual flame; while allegory is one of many possible representations of an embodied thing, and belongs to fancy and not to imagination.[11]

Although discourse about allegory and symbol occurred mainly in literary criticism, one can also apply the distinction to visual art. Owens noted, for example, that the opposition between allegory and symbol is well captured in the difference between history painting and modernist abstraction. Artists like Jacques-Louis David created 'machines' with complex narratives corresponding to contemporaneous concerns; a Modernist like Mondrian or Rothko painted images possessing unity and depth, connoting only aesthetic and spiritual resolution. An allegory does not even try to offer what a Mondrian or Rothko is meant

---

9   Thomas Carlyle, *Sartor Resartus* (Berkeley: University of California Press, 2000 [1836]).

10 Bainard Cowan, 'Walter Benjamin's Theory of Allegory', *New German Critique*, vol 22 (Winter, 1981), 109–122: 111.

11 W.B. Yeats, 'William Blake's Illustrations to the *Divine Comedy*' (1903), in *Essays and Introductions* (London: MacMillan, 1961), 116–145: 116. See Nicholas Halmi, 'Coleridge on Allegory and Symbol', in *The Oxford Handbook of Samuel Taylor Coleridge*, ed. Frederick Burwick (Oxford University Press, 2009), 345–358.

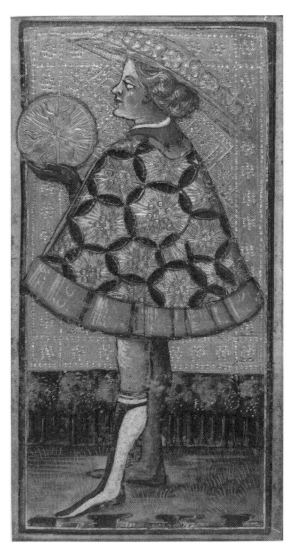

Tarot card – The Knave of Pentacles, c. 1490s. Formerly attributed to Antonio di Ciconagra. Watercolour, varnished, on card. Croft-Lyons Bequest. In the collection of the Victoria and Albert Museum, London. © Victoria and Albert Museum, London

Tarot card – Stella The Knave of Pentacles Death Ace of Cups,
c. 1490s. Formerly attributed to Antonio di Ciconagra.
Watercolour, varnished, on card. Croft-Lyons Bequest.
In the collection of the Victoria and Albert Museum, London.
© Victoria and Albert Museum, London

to provide: a moment of escape, self-sufficient and autonomous. In a symbolic artwork, the very physicality of the artwork may seem to recede, allowing for a moment of heightened response. By contrast, allegory remains resolutely grounded in the material. Its characteristic motion is not a pathway up, but a lateral movement across the interwoven realm of signification. This is why allegory became 'proscribed territory' within Modernism, and conversely, why Owens adopted it as the foundation for his new theory of Postmodernism. He saw the allegorical mode as a way to deny the false promise of 'pure presence', and to re-engage art with the social sphere.[12]

The opposition between symbol and allegory also helps us understand the phenomenon of craft's inferiority within Modernist discourse. As I argued in *Thinking Through Craft*, Modernism was premised on principles of autonomy and optical clarity, principles that were rooted in the Romantic conception of artistic genius.[13] Within such a worldview, craft's supplemental status (that is, its supporting and self-effacing role) and its assertive materiality relegate it to a position outside the pure symbolic order. Yet this relegation was itself contradictory, involving a blindness to the Modernist artwork's physical dependencies on skill, technical traditions and materiality. It seems clear that craft has found a less problematic position within the interdisciplinary and layered condition of Postmodernism. But does this mean that craft is inherently allegorical? That is a more complicated question.

Ornament and rhetoric

We might begin by looking at a concept closely related (but certainly not identical) to craft: ornament. This is a term that recurs throughout discussions on allegory, though to my knowledge, no other recent author has isolated it for special attention. In his essay on the allegorical impulse, Owens emphasized that the mode's 'meta-textual' character is the primary reason for its low reputation and analogized this to the role of ornament: 'Allegory is attacked as interpretation merely appended post facto to a work, a rhetorical ornament or flourish.' Allegory cannot stand on its own, nor does it restore the lost meaning of a

12 Owens, 'The Allegorical Impulse', part one, 81.
13 Glenn Adamson, *Thinking Through Craft* (Oxford: Berg/V&A Publishing, 2007).

text intact. Rather, it is supplemental, in the sense that its metaphor is arbitrarily added, a supervening layer.[14] It is not an autonomous form, but rather something akin to decoration.

Here as elsewhere, our critic was closely following Walter Benjamin's *Origin of German Tragic Drama*, which looms, a melancholic monument, over Owens' essay. To understand the genesis of the 'allegorical impulse', it is essential to engage with this famously difficult text – Benjamin's first book, which was submitted (unsuccessfully) as his habilitation dissertation in 1925, then published two years later to little fanfare, nearly lost, and rediscovered only years after the author's death. The text became widely available to a German readership only in 1955, as part of an edited selection of Benjamin's writings; the English translation appeared in 1977, just in time for Owens to discover it.

Benjamin's project was, on one level, straightforwardly historical, an academic exercise. The brief he set himself was to construct an account of Baroque stage tragedies (*Trauerspiels*, literally 'sorrow plays'). Previous scholarship had not been kind to these seventeenth-century allegorical texts, which are prolix and convoluted, densely crowded precessions of classical and religious allusions, devoid of psychological character development or pleasing narrative shape. In a word, they are boring. Undeterred, Benjamin – who would later pen the famous line, 'boredom is the dream bird that hatches the egg of experience' – set himself the task of retrieving these seemingly remote texts for intellectual history.[15] Rejecting the Romantic rejection, he attributed to them a potentially redemptive significance.

It was here that Benjamin diverged dramatically from expectation, in ways that his university superiors found incomprehensible. Much as Owens would later use Benjamin's text to his own Postmodernist ends, Benjamin projected on to the historical dramas his own tragic worldview. From the outset, he conceded the decadent nature of the

---

14 'If he adds [the allegorist] does so only to replace: the allegorical meaning supplants an antecedent one; it is a supplement. This is why allegory is condemned, but it is also the source of its theoretical significance.' Owens, 'The Allegorical Impulse', part one, 69.

15 Walter Benjamin, 'The Storyteller', 1936; reprinted in *Walter Benjamin: Illuminations*, ed. Hannah Arendt (New York: Schocken, 2007), 96. See Peter Toohey, *Boredom: A Lively History* (New Haven: Yale University Press, 2011); Patricia Meyer Spacks, *Boredom: The Literary History of a State of Mind* (Chicago: University of Chicago Press, 2005).

Baroque, 'not so much an age of genuine artistic achievement as an age possessed of an unremitting artistic will'. He also recognized the fundamental arbitrariness of these allegorical texts, in which 'any person, any object, any relationship can mean absolutely anything else'.[16] Yet – and this will not surprise anyone familiar with Benjamin's unfinished, digressive lifework *The Arcades Project* – he glimpsed in the arbitrariness of allegory a means of continuously confronting the chasm between reality and representation.[17] The potentially infinite succession of metaphorical emblems in allegory, so many pieces of a puzzle that refuse to cohere, were for him an apt reflection of lived experience, which is transitory, often enigmatic, and ultimately of course, leads only to death.[18]

For him, the reassuring wholeness of symbol, its promise of an ironclad meaning bound up in a single resplendent sign, could only be a lie. Allegory was a much truer reflection of the state of affairs. Its ever-accumulating series of signs could bear the weight of actual culture, even if in the aggregate, they could not be taken to 'mean' anything, except for the fact of impermanence itself. As he so often would in his later writings, Benjamin reached for a craft metaphor to convey this idea: 'The value of fragments of thought is all the greater the less direct their relationship to the underlying idea, and the brilliance of the representation depends as much on this value as the brilliance of the mosaic does on the quality of the glass paste.'[19]

In passages like these, Benjamin's allusions to ornament are highly suggestive for our purposes. He painstakingly traced the development of Baroque emblems, tracking their origins in classical texts about

---

16 Benjamin, *Origin of German Tragic Drama*, 54–55; 175.

17 Helen Hills has memorably written that in Benjamin's thinking, 'Allegory betrays the appearance which it sets out to represent; but as that appearance was untrue, allegory opens up the possibility of gaining truth.' Helen Hills, 'The Baroque: The Grit in the Oyster of Art History', in *Rethinking the Baroque*, ed. Hills (Farnham: Ashgate, 2011), 23.

18 See Cowan, 'Walter Benjamin's Theory of Allegory', 110.

19 Benjamin, *Origin of German Tragic Drama*, 29. On Benjamin's use of craft as figurative material, see Esther Leslie, 'Walter Benjamin: Traces of Craft', *Journal of Design History*, vol 11, no. 1 (1998), 5–13. Leslie comments on Benjamin's technique of montage, 'using debris and rubbish, the broken pots and torn scraps, not the high, sublime reordering of harmony in a bloodless, hands-off aestheticism'. (p. 12)

rhetoric, via Renaissance iconological guides, through to the 'richness of extravagance' that so defined the period stylistically: gaudy decoration, twisting columns and triumphal arches, commemorative medallions and coins and elaborate heraldic devices. He wrote, too, of the 'subtle theoretical recipes' of alchemists, suggesting that their hermetic knowledge exemplified the Baroque conception of genius: 'The man of genius, the master of the *ars inveniendi* [arts of invention], is that of a man who could manipulate models with sovereign skill.'[20]

Benjamin knew well that the Baroque's ornamental embellishment and illusionistic virtuosity might seem to ring hollow, but for him, the endless accumulation of details bespoke the desire for meaning more than any direct assertion of meaning could. The critic Michael Taussig summarizes it beautifully: 'Allegory reminds us that by necessity reality skids away from logic, and it is this gap, this apparent imperfection, that nourishes the sacred as the desire for and the impossibility of the union between truth and meaning.'[21] In discussing this 'gap', Benjamin once more fielded an artisanal analogy, which, as he must have seen, applied just as well to his own work as to any seventeenth-century author:

> The writer must not conceal the fact that his activity is one of arranging, since it was not so much the mere whole as its obviously constructed quality that was the principal impression which was aimed at. Hence the display of the craftsmanship, which (...) shows through like the masonry in a building whose rendering has broken away.[22]

It is here that we really arrive at the nexus of allegory and craft. It would not be quite right to say that craft is inherently allegorical. Rather, we might put it like this: it is through craft that allegorical structures are made. (Here I am using the term 'craft' in its least complicated sense, just as skilled work, without the artistic or ideological implications it is often made to carry.) Ornament provides a paradigmatic case: without technique, it is impossible to create the emblematic density that allegory requires. Furthermore, while a symbolic text tends to presume the transcendence (and hence, the denial) of its own facture, the underlying procedures of an allegorical text are always evident.

20 Benjamin, *Origin of German Tragic Drama*, 178, 179.
21 Michael Taussig, 'What Color is the Sacred?', *Critical Inquiry*,
    vol. 33, no. 1 (Autumn 2006), 28–51: 40.
22 Benjamin, *Origin of German Tragic Drama*, 179.

As Benjamin puts it, the structure of the masonry shows through. (This is why Carlyle dismissed it as exhibiting 'the Daub of Artifice'.) This aspect of allegory also has a temporal dimension. If a symbolic form possesses immediacy and can be considered complete once it is realized, an allegorical text is durational. It unfolds over time, potentially without end. As it does so, it continually draws attention to the procedures that give it form. And so, right alongside Owens' examples of appropriation, collage and seriality, we should set craft processes – not because they are inherently allegorical in themselves, but because they are perfectly suited to allegory's conventionalized and elaborate nature.

We can further explore the question of allegory's relation to craft with the help of two further theoretical texts. The first is *Allegory: Theory of a Symbolic Mode* (1964), by the literary critic Angus Fletcher. Though writing independently of Benjamin, Fletcher comes to a similar set of conclusions about the ornamental logic of allegory. Of particular interest is his extended passage on *kosmos*, a Greek term meaning roughly 'orderly arrangement', which Fletcher places at the centre of his analysis. For him, the doubled structure of allegory necessarily implies a relationship between multiple scales. An allegorical text is a microcosm, which captures a larger reality (macrocosm) in a condensed, emblematic manner. Thus for example, George Orwell's *Animal Farm* captures, in simple storybook form, the fateful politics of the Soviet revolution and ensuing regime; similarly, in *The Handmaid's Tale,* Margaret Atwood imagines a dystopian future that encapsulates present gender relations in exaggerated form.

Building on this observation, Fletcher makes the excellent point, not particularly emphasized by Benjamin, that allegory is often employed to assert authority. Its 'cosmic' (ordering) role is to establish an overall hierarchical structure through the amassing of innumerable details. Pointing to the examples of Baroque churches, medieval banners and coats of arms – which of course were achieved through the crafts of stonework, sewing and armoury – he notes that such allegorical constructs have the primary function of asserting rank within a system. This is essentially a conservative purpose, which cannot work without a well-established and widely understood visual code. 'The old saws of religion and morality need far more than mere illustration to bring them to life', he writes. 'They need their own proper ornaments, the signs that go with them systematically, as the vestments of the priest go with the Mass, or the insignia of his uniform go with the military dictator or five-star general.'[23]

Fletcher also raises a related point that has to do with the emotional pitch of allegory. The Romantics (and following them, the Modernists) believed that only an imaginative and expressive symbol could stir profound feeling. Fletcher disputes this: 'Nothing could be more likely to arouse intense emotional response than the status symbol.'[24] For all that an allegorical system may seem tedious from an external point of view – its encoded references, heraldic signs, or repetitive allusions to Classical mythology – for those operating within an allegorical system, it can be highly affective. This in turn helps to explain its rhetorical power.

Fletcher's commentary is useful in that it directs our attention to craft's more normative aspects – its compatability with conventional and even authoritarian tendencies. Too often, modern proponents of craft have embraced it as a guarantor of individualism. Yet that presumption, put forward so forcefully in the writings of William Morris, is at variance with much of actual craft practice. Even the most cursory glance at decorative art history is enough to remind us that high levels of skill have often been employed, anonymously and repetitively, to assert the privileges of high status and to furnish the trappings of power. Craftsmanship is also often called into service in religious ceremonial contexts, where devotion to labour is meant to reflect spiritual devotion. Allegory certainly can be used satirically, as Orwell and Atwood show, but more often it serves to indicate straightforward allegiance: consider the use of feudal medieval banners (or for that matter contemporary protest banners, which employ similar

---

23 Angus Fletcher, *Allegory: The Theory of a Symbolic Mode* (Ithaca: Cornell University Press, 1964), 120. See also p. 116, note 74.

24 Fletcher, *Allegory*, 117. Some pages later, he picks up this theme: 'There are innumerable cases and kinds of ornamental art which need to be analyzed for their double meaning, their "cosmic" meaning: Anglo-Saxon poetry, its imagery all "curiously inwrought"; the ornaments of baroque poetry, as well as baroque music and architecture; the rococo facades of churches; the mazy twirls and hidden dells of picturesque art and landscape gardening (…) all these and innumerable other instances of ornament could be shown to imply, within an emotively charged system of beliefs, a hierarchical system.'

visual tropes to contrary but equally ideological effect).[25] Fletcher's discussion of embellishment within allegorical systems – the details that signify the macrocosm – helps us to see how craft can operate powerfully, in an entirely non-individualistic manner.

A final, more recent theoretical text that deserves attention here is 'Riegl's *Mache*', by the art historian Christopher S. Wood. Published in the journal *RES* in 2004, it is a closely argued profile of the *fin de siècle* curator and historian Alois Riegl, focused particularly on his studies of ancient jewellery. While Wood does not focus as much on allegory as the other authors reviewed here, he does offer a novel interpretation of craft that is highly relevant to our discussion. In a pattern that should now be familiar (and which I am aware of replicating myself, here), Wood claims to be interpreting Riegl, while actually offering an innovative account of his own. He begins by reviewing the lowly status of jewellery within the discipline of art history, on account of its supplemental character: 'Idealist aesthetics could be characterized as one long process of delegitimization of the raw appeal of metal and gem', he writes. Jewellery could 'never accede to the autonomy, self containedness, or self-sufficiency of the artwork (...) The wrought form collapses inward on itself and is not redeemed by a concept'.[26]

Despite his deep interest in decorative art, Wood says, Riegl took this supplementary, 'unthinking' status for granted. Yet, rather as Benjamin found a redemptive possibility in the repetitive metaphor of Baroque drama, Riegl saw an unexpected potency in jewellery's actual making, its *Mache* (German for 'fabrication' or 'artifice', roughly equivalent to the Greek *techne*).[27] Building on Riegl's book *Late Roman Art Industry* (*Die spätrömische Kunst-Industrie*, 1901), as well as Angus Fletcher's conception of ornament as allegorical and intrinsically hierarchical, Wood writes of jewellery as 'establishing rank in a hierarchy that was analogically related to the cosmos'. Crucially though, he differs from Fletcher in locating the source of empathic potential in the

---

25 See Glenn Adamson, 'Anatomy of the Protest Banner', *Disegno* (September/October 2017).

26 Christopher S. Wood, 'Riegl's *Mache*', *RES: Anthropology and Aesthetics 46* (Autumn, 2004), 154–172: 158, 155.

27 It should be noted that there is also a direct historiographical connection here, as Benjamin is known to have read Riegl with interest. See Margaret Iversen: *Alois Rigel: Art History and Theory* (Cambridge, MA: MIT Press, 1993).

Kari Steihaug: *Ruin*, 2007. Installation, 700×125 cm, hand-knitted wool garments, thread, steel. Photo: Thor Westrebø. Courtesy: KODE Art Museums and Composer Homes, Bergen.

act of fabrication. He sees jewellery as asserting its function through its essential materiality: its very 'wroughtness', as he puts it, 'the spectacle of metal submitted to folding, bending, chiselling, puncturing, and scratching'.[28] Jewellery does not posit a viewer in the way that a painting or play does. It is not dependent on a separation from the everyday. Rather, it sits within the flow of materiality, simply attracting and intensifying our attention.[29]

Retracing the same historical progression that Benjamin and Owens identified, Wood goes on to argue that jewellery has been sidelined, not only because of its supplementarity, but also because it operates through what might be called a materialist metaphor:

> The mind that prized the artifact as a talisman or a link to a higher sphere of the cosmos is figured as a phenomenon of the past. The modern mind then has the choice of whether to go back and seek authenticity in that origin, or to leave the origin safely behind. The modern relationship to the artifact is always presented as comparatively disengaged, abstract, and intellectualized. This is a virtually universal feature of the modern approach to object-quality (...) Art history assimilated at an early stage and has never really abandoned the ideal-historical schema of a primordial 'tactile' relationship to artifacts that through history is transformed into an intellectualized or spiritualized 'optical' relationship. I would say that the analysis of artifacts in art historical writing, whether it is framed as formalist or contextualist, always proceeds within this historicist transformatory schema.[30]

Wood here emphasizes the physicality of the allegorical 'talisman', and the gulf that has widened between art history as a discipline and the literal objects of its study. Also important in this passage is the fate of the originary past, which, he argues, is typically either fetishized by the historian, in the form of nostalgia, or held at a remove, where it can safely be subjected to study. The modern mind seeks to understand the past, but not to actually hold it close.

---

28 Wood, 'Riegl's *Mache*', 161.

29 This conception of allegorical ornament again accords with Walter Benjamin's: 'It is common in the literature of the Baroque to pile up fragments ceaselessly, without any strict idea of a goal, and in the unremitting expectation of a miracle, to take the repetition of stereotypes for a process of intensification.' *Origin of German Tragic Drama*, 178.

30 Wood, 'Riegl's *Mache*', 163–164.

This separation from the past is exactly the distance that Benjamin was trying to cross. He argued that allegory is by its very nature a rearrangement of existing, often ancient material: 'Allegories are, in the realm of thoughts, what ruins are in the realm of things.' He pictured his Baroque texts as layered and labyrinthine (this again stands in contrast to symbol, which typically presents itself as a flash of new insight). They did constitute a type of history, but 'history as a petrified, primordial landscape', which one might wander through in search of meaning, but never comprehend as a totality.[31] Benjamin sought precisely to establish a way of summoning the past in a manner that is not 'disengaged, abstract, and intellectualized', but infused with dramatic revelation – this is the famous 'tiger's leap' (*Tigersprung*) that has become so associated with him.[32] Allegory, a premodern means of representing things that are emotionally charged, concrete and sensuous, provides a possible framework for the past to be redeemed.

Ruin and repetition

The history of modern craft suggests the difficulty of this goal. The choice that Wood delineates – either reconstruct the past in a spirit of nostalgia, or leave any sense of origin behind – well describes the tension inherent within craft movements, their tendencies toward revival on the one hand, and avant-garde exploration on the other. The path of allegory, as convoluted as it may be, offers a third way. This is not exactly a new idea; we should remember that John Ruskin, the first modern theorist to call for a return to the premodern, was a great lover of ruins, as of course was Benjamin.[33] It is easy to be critical of the nineteenth-century craft revivalists' ambition to restore medieval patterns of life and work in ways that were frankly impossible (indeed,

31 Benjamin, *Origin of German Tragic Drama*, 178, 166.
32 Ulrich Lehmann, *Tigersprung: Fashion in Modernity* (Cambridge, MA: MIT Press, 2000).
33 Andrew Spurr has interpreted the dispute between Ruskin and Viollet-le-Duc – the great preservationist and the great rebuilder of monuments – in relation to the distinction between symbol and allegory: 'On one hand, the timeless unity of the object with its ideal essence; on the other hand, rupture, disunity, and the pathos evoked by the material remains of an irrecoverable past.' David Spurr, *Architecture and Modern Literature* (Ann Arbor: University of Michigan Press, 2012), 158.

I myself have been critical of them on just this score).[34] Their efforts did often prompt shallow nostalgia.[35] Yet if we strip away narrow revivalism, we can see that their ambition to reconnect with the past without falsifying it, lies right at the heart of modern craft. In allegory, we see how this can be done: through forms of practice that are open-ended, repetitive and inconclusive. These forms of practice allude to premodern ways of making without trying literally to reproduce them; they avoid the easy gratifications of symbolism and instead embrace the complexity of 'continuous metaphor'. They are assertively material, and yet contain cosmic implications.

These thoughts bring us back full circle to Craig Owens' essay 'The Allegorical Impulse'. For, as much as he was concerned with typically Postmodern artistic strategies, cerebral rather than artisanal in their methods, he was also animated by a desire for emotional connection, no less genuine than that of Ruskin or Morris. In subsequent years, it is worth pointing out, Owens would be one of the formative influences on artists engaged with 'identity politics', writing with particular passion on topics relating to gay selfhood and the impact of AIDS (from which he himself died in 1990).[36] Returning to his essay, therefore, it is no surprise to find a psychological intensity coursing under the surface of his erudition. The clue is in the title: he was concerned not just with allegory, but also with *impulse*. He saw that the structures employed by Hanne Darboven or Sol LeWitt, for example, were not only propositions about artistic ontology; they also could be read as expressions of 'obsessional neurosis'. What principally attracted him to Benjamin's theory, perhaps, was its emotional tenor, the possibility that yearning and melancholy could themselves be the basis of an operative technique. Hence Owens' dramatic phrasing, in describing the promise of the allegory as its 'capacity to rescue from historical oblivion that which threatens to disappear', through 'a *conviction* of the remoteness of the past, and a *desire* to redeem it for the present'.[37]

---

34 Glenn Adamson, *The Invention of Craft* (London: Bloomsbury, 2013), ch. 4.

35 See Edward S. Cooke, Jr., 'The Long Shadow of William Morris: Paradigmatic Problems of Twentieth-Century American Furniture', in *The Craft Reader,* ed. Glenn Adamson (London: Bloomsbury, 2010).

36 For his later writings, see Craig Owens, *Beyond Recognition: Representation, Power, and Culture* (Berkeley: University California Press, 1994).

37 Owens, 'The Allegorical Impulse', part one, 68. The italics here are mine.

It has often been said that Walter Benjamin's thought anticipated Postmodernism. *The Origin of German Tragic Drama* does seem eerily prescient of 1980s art and literature – even at the basic level of its writerly qualities, its myriad collaged quotations and sudden disjunctions. It is also clear that Benjamin's retrieval of the Baroque offers routes back to premodern values which were, as Owens puts it, 'foreclosed' in a Modernist paradigm. What may be less obvious is that allegory, as Benjamin describes it, allows for a convergence of the pre-modern *and* the Postmodern. He bequeathed us a way to think through issues of historical return: how to avoid the traps of nostalgia or the fetishization of the new, to understand the past as past while still finding a way to make it present.

For those of us who have an interest in craft, the discourse I have charted here suggests a set of principles for approaching what Wood calls the 'wroughtness' of artefacts. Yielding to the allegorical impulse means abandoning 'disengaged, abstract, and intellectualized' approaches. It means valuing the intricate involutions of crafted things, not unpicking them through analysis. It means that we should not equate craft to individualism, or attempt to elevate it to the status of art, as a symbolic order might imply; but instead recognize it as a means of generating deeply inscribed, if often hierarchical, cultural arrangements. And it means recognizing the emotional affect that is embedded in these same crafted artefacts, simply by virtue of their place in an ongoing chain of human association.

It may seem odd to have arrived at these primary insights through a series of abstruse theoretical writings. But, for all that they have been placed in opposition to one another over the years, theory and craft are actually ideal partners. Theory helps us adjust our intuitions, infusing them with a higher degree of intelligence; in craft, intelligence is grounded and (one might say) dispersed into the material domain. Just as it is always helpful to enlarge the meaning of objects through interpretation, ideas should be continually tested against the reality of practice. Thinking through craft, you see, is a two-way street.

Ja Kyung Shin: *Finger lickin' spoons,* 2013. Ag 925, electro-formed, mounted.
Photo: KC Studio

An Emotional Perspective
on Everyday Use

Anders Ljungberg

Functional objects bear images of us as users and as human beings. A glass gets its form – quite obviously, one might think – from the need to be able to be grabbed and lifted, from the shape of our mouths, and from the amount of liquid we need to drink on a given occasion. The glass has, then, a direct relationship to our bodies and their proportions. But this glass, through recurrent, widespread use, has also been laden with more metaphorical and, on another level, emotional meanings. Using these bodily relations and metaphorical and emotional meanings as points of departure, I attempt in this text to highlight different situations of use; that is to say, the event that occurs when a user, in a given spatial context, and from her or his specific physical, mental and cultural preconditions, sets the object in motion, thereby fulfilling its purpose as a functional object and, in so doing, also defines himself or herself as an artefact-using human.[1] All the use of objects that takes place in daily life, and which has taken place since the appearance of the first functional object, has imbued these objects with our ideas about them. While this has led to the objects finding their best form for a given purpose, it has also meant that we, in the process of developing them, have placed our care and our dreams into their development and use. Functional objects carry traces of human identity that can perhaps only be seen in the objects themselves. In the daily use of these objects – a use we all participate in – values are called forth and reflect our image of ourselves. When we drink, we do so from a vessel and allow the liquid to be transported to another vessel: ourselves. This is a silent event in which the glass drafted into use gives us the liquid, which, with its coolness, outlines the inner image of ourselves. This

---

1   See Maurice Merleau-Ponty, *Phenomenology of Perception*. (London: Routledge, 2013), 171–177.

description of an instance of use lies closer to poetry than that which we can find in the rational and practically-oriented view of consumption that reigned during the functionalist twentieth century.

A bowl, perhaps an overused metaphor in the context of craft, has often been put forth as a metaphor for the body. What I also find interesting in this context is that an empty bowl, stemming from our conception of a bowl as full, is loaded with expectations and a desire to be filled. If we inspect the relationship between ourselves and functional objects, there are many examples showing how the objects carry images of us; in this case, our desires. This relationship to objects is an example of an outwardly emotional approach in which the bowl's practical function as a container for, say, apples is not its central function. The instances of use described above demonstrate a kind of intimacy in which a user and an object become one.[2] We are not always aware of this intimacy because our daily lives are largely characterized by the fact that we are always orienting ourselves to what comes next. As we do not give ourselves time to reflect on the inherent, sometimes hidden qualities of objects, this intimacy and presence do not become visible to us during instances of use.

Much of this daily use takes place in silence, in the sense that an instance of use does not need to be described in words or be defined concretely in order for us to complete it and incorporate it into our daily lives. We regard what we do in our daily use as self-evident. Habit hides from us the value that such events can have. Perhaps this is as it should be, but through a greater focus on presence, it may be that we can more fully understand our lives through these instances of use and through other silent components in our daily lives, rather than through our identity as consumers.

---

2   Several ideas are contained in the notion of the intimacy of an object and its material. In order to understand the ideas, we must take into account experiences of our own bodies. When our hands, mouth or other body parts come in contact with a functional object, it gives of its materiality and form. Through such a process, we understand and are made aware of our own physical presence. This encounter is intimate largely because it takes place beyond all intellectual models of explanation (which create distance in themselves). Intimate communication between an individual user and an individual functional object arises on a completely wordless plane.

Anders Ljungberg: *Into,* 2008. Silver, zink, corian. 12 × 15 × 19 cm.
In the collection of Designmuseum Röhhska, Gothenburg.
Photo: Håkansson/Mannberg

In my work as a crafts practitioner and designer, I have found several values embedded in the daily use of objects. These values are part of what constructs everyone's daily life, even if the use itself can vary depending on class, gender, culture, age and so on. What I attempt to describe in this essay is therefore a phenomenon all of us are aware of, even if we do not name it or give it any space, in a time when the consumption of objects is valued more than their use.

Functional objects

In this section, I attempt to describe how functional objects can be the basis for a discussion that focuses on the emotional aspects of their use. This will be grounded primarily on a discussion around a vessel (here represented by a pitcher/carafe), partly because the vessel can be said to include interesting features with regard to its emotionally charged use, but also because it lies close to my own experience as a silversmith and designer.

Openings

One prerequisite for a vessel to be able to share its contents with us as users and the given environment is that it must have an opening. A vessel with no opening is closed; it makes itself inaccessible to us and maintains its interior without being able to give anything to itself or its surroundings.

An object may have different kinds of openings, and openings give us different kinds of information about the sort of object we are dealing with. What makes a bowl a bowl is that it is completely open to its surroundings (it holds space), while the inside of a bottle, unless it is made of glass, can only be reached in our imagination. This closedness or openness influences our perception of the object as a generous participant in its surroundings (inclusive) or as closed and unreachable (but giving). To a certain extent, we also relate emotionally to an object based on its intended use. We probably experience a vase that closes itself around its inner space in a different way than we experience a pitcher. The essence of the vase is precisely that it takes the place of an underground water source that nourishes the roots of a plant; it references the plant as a thing that grows in the earth and draws water out from the earth's inner structures. The pitcher, on the other hand, is based on the principle of giving, and the source to which it refers is generous in character, regardless of whether, depending on its construction, we associate it with something open (a carafe) or an underground source (a vase).

Even the edge around a vessel's opening influences its relationship to itself and to space. An inward or outward curve gives us an understanding of an object as closed or open to its surroundings. The use of a vessel to pour, for example, changes the direction of its opening relative to the space around it. The mouth of a carafe, which is directed upward in space before pouring begins, changes in the stages of pouring and starts pointing in different directions. This is amplified and traced by the stream created in the process of pouring the contents of the carafe. The same can be said for human speech: we trace the dimensions of space by pointing our voice in different directions. The stream is the carafe's voice, and it carries and conveys the carafe's internal values to the surrounding world.[3]

Details

Spouts, handles, lids, buttons, serrations... various details on an item create its distinctive character as a functional object. These details convey to us as users the ways in which it wants to be used.[4]

When we take in, classify and manipulate an object through action, we usually do so in light of on our previous experiences in similar situations and through interaction with similar objects. This previous experience and the enormous knowledge-base that all of these encounters have created means that we usually do not need to ponder very much before we understand how to behave in relation to most of the objects we encounter in everyday life. Their details draw both our physical and mental understanding into an activity in agreement with the objects. All functional details on objects tend to have a conventional location, which means that we not only know quickly how we should act, but that we also do so without questioning the situation to any great extent. The chain of agreements between our intellect, our body and the functional object that results in action takes place in silence and without us paying further attention to it. This is probably fortunate if we are

---

3   See Gaston Bachelard, *Water and Dreams* (Dallas: Dallas Institute of Humanities and Culture, 1999), 187–196.

4   For a deeper discussion on this that involves the concept of 'affordance', see James J. Gibson, *The Ecological Approach to Visual Perception* (Boston: Houghton, 1979).

David Clarke: *In Flux,* 2012. Silver. Photo: David Clarke

to be functional individuals in society. It should be pointed out, however, that what might be considered a functioning member of society is exclusionary, since these functional details only apply to a limited range of functional variations, and this normativity is reinforced in every instance of use.[5]

The functional details, as described above, get their form from their intended use. A handle gives us predetermined and exact instructions for gripping, and a spout shows us the generous principle of pouring with its opening and shape. But is it the case that the spout can be understood as generous only because of our previous experience of spouts, or is there something obviously generous in its form? Perhaps it is impossible to say whether its form arose from our emotional experience of pouring, combined with all the sacred rituals of human history, etcetera, or whether it evolved based on a practical, functional orientation. These two perspectives have been intimately interwoven, since in our quotidian use, they become unified in our perception, both in emotional and practical terms. The spout's generosity has formed our language, even if we do not perceive it in our everyday lives. For example, in Swedish, the word denoting a pitcher is *tillbringare*, which describes not only the object but also the user and the action. It points to a generous act, to bring something forth, quite literally.

Grip and availability

One detail guiding us in the use of an object is its handle. There can be different reasons why we put handles on functional objects. Most obviously, they prevent us from burning ourselves on hot mugs, for example, or they give us a sturdier grip, especially when the objects are fairly large. Handles also gives us a defined grip, a clear instruction. This instruction, however, may mean that we do not examine the objects further with our hands, other than by the suggested gripping. In this way, a handle can distance us from an object. We are prevented from fully integrating it into our physical space.

If we are forced to involve our body when using a larger vessel, another kind of communication emerges between the object and

---

5   Sara Ahmed, *Queer Phenomenology, Orientations, Objects, Others* (Durham and London: Duke University Press, 2006), 47–51.

Anders Ljungberg: *Handled #1*, 2011. Silver, used handles (mixed materials), 150 × 130 × 170 mm. Photo: Håkansson/Mannberg

ourselves as users. The way in which it is held and its size are decisive factors in how we incorporate it into our embodied life. To pour from a large vessel without a handle require us to use our entire body, a motion which describes us in a different way than does our use of a coffee cup, which we touch and control precisely with our fingers.

Objects and contents

An optimal spout is considered to be one that pours in an even stream and does not drip on the tablecloth. This, of course, is a functionalist perspective on the concept of function.[6] From another perspective, one could argue that the optimal spout is one that creates a gurgling sound and drips on the tablecloth in order to emphasize the activity which has just taken place. The gurgling and dripping describe the character of the pitcher, the liquid and the pouring. This could be described as a more poetic perspective on the concept of function.

The relationship between an object and its contents creates conditions for several interesting considerations, since the contents (food, water, coffee, etc.) greatly contribute to the overall expression of the object (the coffee heats the coffee pot, the wine makes the crystal carafe red and gives it a different balance and weight). We can see how, throughout history, vessels describe their intended contents in various ways, often with decorative symbols, but also through having forms that are more directly related to their contents. One of the most blatant examples of the content/vessel relationship is a water bag, one of the oldest ways to transport water. The water bag is often made out of the stomach or skin of an animal.

The 'form' of the bag, or, if one prefers, the vessel, is hidden from us until it is filled with water. In this case, the water is not subordinate to the object but rather a collaborator in the overall expression of the water bag. When we manipulate and hold the full bag, we can also sense the pressure of the water from its inside in the same way that we

---

6   During the twentieth century, the concept of function came to be unquestionably associated with a practically oriented view of function. Going further back (to the silverware of the Baroque era, for example), one can see the function of objects as primarily social in nature. In yet other contexts, one could speak of aesthetic or communicative functions. In today's society, it is possible to regard all of these concepts of function as more important than an object's practical function.

sense the inner pressure in a body. In this symbiotic relationship, the hierarchy between object and subject is suspended.[7]

Empathy for an object

What, then, are the elements of an object that create a desire in us to use it? As mentioned above, this desire may be created partly through the object's openings and its relationship to space, its relation to itself and to ourselves as users. But there are also other aspects which invite or perhaps discourage us from using the given object.

One of these aspects is our ability to identify with the object based on its shape. In the twentieth century, we saw a development, even within the arts, of objects which adhere to industrialism and its desire to create a rational aesthetic, in the sense that the intended use and the object's creation story are not hidden under mystical questions or challenging messages. In other words: the object's value lies only in solving a practical problem in a situation of use, without us asking any questions about this use. Also in the twentieth century, even objects created through an artistic process increasingly took on a mechanical expression, as a rationalist aesthetic was prized in the industrial world. This aesthetic was the result of simplified production processes and a uniformity of expression with the goal of reaching as many potential consumers as possible. It is likely that this has also partly shaped our ideas about how we want the things around us to look, which also means that when we formulate our concepts about the expression of objects, we do so from generalized and rationalized preconceptions and not from our dreams about the objects. Has this rational aesthetic created distance between us and the intended functional objects? If so, could that mean that we, in this distance, appear more clearly as humans and users precisely in contrast to machines and mechanically made things? I believe, in any case, that it is possible to argue that our empathy for and recognition of the objects as being part of the same organic structure as we are, changes when we can identify with them. This empathy may create the preconditions for different degrees of desire to use things and to participate in the world of things.

---

7   See the chapter 'Water' in Francis Ponge, *The Voice of Things*
    (New York: McGraw-Hill, 1974), 49–51. Available at
    https://www.scribd.com/doc/56540549/Francis-Ponge-The-Voice-of-Things
    (accessed 16 November 2017).

Anders Ljungberg: *Bag Beneath #1*, 2016. Silver, deconstructed bureau,
18 × 16 × 25 cm. Photo: Anders Ljungberg

Relationship to the ground and space

The usual relationship between a functional object and the base on which it rests is that of a flat bottom meeting a flat table. Because the interface between them is seamless, the object sits firmly on the table's surface. This also means that the object can be perceived as belonging to the table and, perhaps not to the same extent, to the room where the user is located. In other words, the object can belong to another object to which it relates to different degrees – in this case, to the table or the room. In the same way, an object not directly attached to a surface can, to a greater degree, entice the intended user to grab it and relate it to himself or herself and the space in which he or she is moving. This may be important in the case of cutlery, for example, as it is intended to be lifted. It should therefore perhaps not lie completely flat on the surface. Cutlery does not belong primarily to the table, but to the hand and mouth. When an object is freed from the surface of the table in this way, an activated space between the object and the table surface emerges, which is different from when the flat surface passively connects to the flat bottom of the object.

My works often take their starting point in ongoing everyday life. When working with them, a number of transformations in materials, spaces and objects take place. My method has often been to distinguish objects from the everyday life from which they originate. I usually do this by placing them in a gallery context. Through this dislocation, it is possible to glimpse the life hidden by the numbing repetition of habit and, hopefully, to discover something important about being and becoming a person.

Understanding an object

The viewing and understanding of an object can be described as layered: we peel away the layers from an object, ultimately to come to its core, its full meaning, and incorporate it into our own activities. How this uncovering takes place is of course completely dependent on what we already know about the object in question. We use most of the objects in our surroundings without needing to put much effort into understanding how they should be used or what it is we are dealing with. We have stored a large amount of information that we use in every tiny action. All of us, at some point, have had to create concepts about the objects and their intended use. We have tasted, felt, waved, squeezed and so forth, thus to bring out the essence of an object for ourselves, but perhaps not always its actual practical meaning.

Even if we know how the steel of a hammer tastes, how the wood of its handle feels against our cheek, and how different the temperatures of wood and steel are, this does not mean that we know how the hammer should be used.[8] No doubt part of this knowledge arises when we wave the hammer around and happen to hit something (in the worst case, ourselves), but this knowledge often requires additional information from elsewhere. It is not easy to make the connection between the nail and the hammer, regardless of how much we might know about the hammer's taste and weight. One condition for truly understanding the inherent worth of an object and the nature of its material is to use of all our senses. Our perception of the hammer is connected with knowing how the steel of its head tastes, how we feel in our body when it hits its target, how it sounds, how we focus on the head of the nail, and how it smells when steel meets steel (even if the hammer is not necessarily something we directly associate with scent). The hammer is therefore not only a practical tool for pounding nails, but also a bearer of memories, scents, tastes and feelings.

A functional object as a bearer of memories

Objects, and perhaps first and foremost the instances of use that occur with them, can evoke memories in a number of ways, as most of us likely have experienced. A particular memory and the feelings associated with it can be uncovered through a sound, a scent or perhaps when we touch a particular surface. In comparison with the memories we can call forth with the help of sight, the memories evoked by our other senses are sometimes hidden from us and can appear suddenly without us being prepared for them. Sight is usually described as the most important sense for gaining information and for taking action, but the question is whether the other senses are not even more important when it comes to evoking memories and feelings. They bypass the filters we have constructed through the numerous images and other visual impressions that wash over us in our visually oriented society. Perhaps in most cases, we think of functional objects as bearers of memories on a metaphorical and psychological plane. A more tangible, physical example of this is the slow wear and tear that occurs through all the hands and mouths and so forth that have come into contact with the object. Wear and tear is a type of record that is conveyed into the hands of future users.

---

8   Ahmed, *Queer Phenomenology*, 47.

Dimensions and credibility

Throughout life, we humans change on many levels. The most concrete changes are perhaps physical. We are born small and grow to the size we reach as adults. This, however, is not true of the objects around us. Certainly, there are functional objects customized for children, but most of the things in our surroundings are larger for us as children than they are later in life. The chair we flop into as adults was one we had to climb onto as children. The table that we as adults put things on and sit at to eat a meal is perhaps something we as children would rather sit under to create a fort. What seems to be the same chair or the same table are, from this point of view, different chairs and different tables, depending on our perspective and the way our bodies create conditions for approaching them. Therefore: the relationship between the dimensions of our bodies and the dimensions of the objects around us changes with the different phases of life.

The beliefs we build up in our perceptions of an object throughout life give us an overall idea about the object's credibility, through aspects such as material, dimensions, weight and so on. A teacup in heavy stoneware, a glass made of thin crystal, a solid spade handle... what are the particular requirements we have of an object and its material dimensions? On what are these requirements and expectations based? Many of the expectations we have of an object come from its intended function. The handle and blade of a spade should be sturdily constructed so that its material, size and structure can manage its task: to dig. When we see the spade, we use our previous experiences to assess whether we believe it can fulfil its purpose. The spade must evoke a sense of credibility. This credibility is generated by our impression of the spade, not its actual strength. Our position, then, is largely based on aspects that are more emotional than strictly scientific.

A champagne glass should be thin in order to emphasize the beverage's crispness and feeling of exclusivity. Various functional objects have therefore been given their dimensions and shape not only based on ergonomic considerations and strength requirements, but also in order to describe, poetically, the earth, the beverage, the fruit or whatever else the item is intended to be used for. Different dimensions give us different perceptions of quality and credibility based on a long history created in our own and others' previous interactions with similar objects.

Myra Mimlitsch-Gray: *Studies in enamelware*, 2014–2016. Group shot.
All objects fabricated in steel. Coated in vitreous, porcelain enamel.
Photo: Myra Mimlitsch-Gray

Myra Mimlitsch-Gray: *Magnification: Engraving*, 2017. Silver,
39,4 cm (diameter) × 6,6 cm (high). Photo: Myra Mimlitsch-Gray

David Bielander: *Paper Bag (Sugar)*, 2016. Patinated silver. Photo: Dirk Eisel

Use

I have thus far indicated several aspects of functional objects that generate emotional experiences of them. I will now focus on the use of these objects and the consequences of that use. What we call *use* involves several actions that, in concert, lead us into a user-situation: the user, the object and the surrounding space are united in a silent agreement aimed at carrying out an event.

Pouring

As with other instances of use, pouring assumes a user. This user is included in a specific pattern of motion that is based on the character and location of the pouring object in which space, the object and the user are united in a common goal – in this case, to pour. The pouring motion can of course differ depending on the vessel's character with regard to size, shape, form and the placement of the handle, as well as the user's position relative to the vessel, the receiving vessel's placement, and so on. A common condition for all pouring events, however, is gravity. The substance being poured streams downward (toward the centre of the earth), just like all substances, which means that in order to pour, we must be able to lift the pouring vessel and its contents to a level above the receiving object. Furthermore, the liquid in the vessel must extend over the vessel's outlet, often called a spout, which is to say, the channel that leads the contents of the vessel outwards. These are seemingly obvious observations, but they are, in fact, the only necessary conditions for pouring to take place. This means that the way the pouring happens and the different ways it involves the user can vary greatly in appearance. Once again, we can quite easily imagine these different stages – in this case the manoeuvring of a liquid between different vessels – as a metaphor for human waiting, longing, emptiness, fullness, passion, and so on.

The principle of pouring has been used in several historical contexts as a metaphor for generosity, flow and the emotion of ecstasy. Uncountable are the fountains that more or less relentlessly indulge in this flowing. This out-pouring belongs not only to religious rites and pompous works of art history but, above all, to our everyday lives. From the moment we get up in the morning – when we pour juice, turn the knobs of the faucet, and so on – our bodies take part in this motion that moves liquid from one place to another. The generosity and principle of giving that are at the root of pouring are why it so naturally became

Anders Ljungberg: *Passages #2*. Silver, steel (partly tinplated) corian.
Photo: Anders Ljungberg

a part of different rituals and why it has been used so extensively in art history. But the same generosity and beauty are actually part of the quotidian pouring which we most often brush past in order to drink what we have poured in the next stage of action. Nevertheless, the pouring event which we take part in as users, along with the vessel and liquid, is an act that is deeply loaded with generosity – a generosity that directs itself toward us in a closed everyday ritual.

In pouring, a stream forms that creates a link between the giving and receiving parties. It is like a temporary bridge between them. The stream also illustrates a direction in the space that makes us conscious not only of the stream and the act of pouring itself, but also of the space in which it is taking place. This direction begins to be outlined as soon as the thought of pouring arises in the user's consciousness, since, from the pitcher's construction and placement, it is approached from a specific direction in order to be grasped by its handle.[9] The idea of the pitcher begins here, separate from the pitcher as an object, since it is the appearance and placement of it that creates the conditions for the user's action.

Filling

Pouring means that something is being filled. This something is usually a receiving vessel (a glass or a body), but it can also be the earth and, at a later stage, plants, when they are watered in the garden. The look of the recipient of pouring, also its water-holding character, create within us different understandings of the pouring event. Our understanding of the event is also based on a predefined idea of how the instance of use should look. When a glass is to be filled, it is undoubtedly regarded as a failure if we pour the liquid onto the table next to the glass (however beautiful the pattern created by the liquid on the tablecloth). This sense of failure is based on the conventional image of how a vessel, a liquid and a user ought to behave. When we complete the expected action, we once again describe ourselves as users in full compliance with all the conventional images that this entails. We add another brick to our quotidian building.

---

9   For a discussion on the body as object and mechanistic
      physiology, see Merleau-Ponty, *Phenomenology of Perception.*

Upon filling, the liquid outlines the structure and form of the receiving party. When it is filled, the glass is described by its interior. That which was previously a part of the air filling the rest of the room in which the glass is located becomes separated from the room's 'air' by the liquid and, in so doing, also concretizes the interior of the glass, achieving its intended purpose. The same happens when we drink. The liquid fills and outlines our interior, which is impossible to perceive visually, but all the more tactile when the liquid's temperature and movement make us aware of our inner shape. Another form of illustration emerges if we pour water onto the earth, as the water distributes itself in the earth and reveals to us a structure that was not entirely visible before, like a slow-moving drawing.

Holding
Viewed from the perspective of its intended function, an empty vessel is a vessel waiting to be filled. In its anticipation, it carries the surrounding space inside it. The vessel holds[10] its contents in a motionless anticipation of the next stage. In this anticipation, the contents of the vessel are charged with an energy that also characterizes the vessel as it prepares itself for the next phase when it will leave its place and continue the journey toward the next stopping point. The intrusive fullness of the inner space, in its pressure against the walls of the vessel, effects a certain threat to the vessel, but it also creates hope out of the knowledge of the impending relief through the emptying of the vessel.

The choreography of use
A functional object exists and is created by being included in an activity. This activity presupposes a user who, in different ways, puts the item to its intended use. All of this takes place in some kind of spatial context. The three components – object, user and space – operate together to create that which characterizes an instance of use. If any of these components are lacking, the *use event* does not take place in full. The object cannot be described as fully functional before it encounters the user and space. The shape taken by the agreement

---

10 The word 'hold' implies both the vessel's function of holding the liquid back from the outer sphere, as well as the more time-oriented meaning of holding the liquid until the next event.

between these components may look completely different depending on the character and placement of the object, the social context, the conditions of the space and the user's previous experiences and circumstances. When, in a particular situation, we enter an instance of use, a choreography of use emerges. We gesture, grab, move and create directions and movements in the space in a way that resembles choreography, except that there is no choreographer. The choreography has emerged completely through our quotidian action. This choreography recurs daily, in many cases. The breakfast we make in the morning (if we do not grab a latte on the road) produces the same kind of choreography day after day. The placement of the milk in the refrigerator requires a particular motion in order to get it to the table; the filling of the teakettle requires another motion. These motions and the movements between the different places and levels in the space work together to make us who we are, to a large extent. A large part of our lives consists of this choreography. This choreography describes our bodies and ourselves.

Das Schweizer Gold – Die Deutsche Mark 1983. Details of the individual pieces:
Das Schweizer Gold 1983. Brooch: paper, acrylic glass, steel, 24 × 8.5 × 4.3 cm.
Edition of 24. *Die Deutsche Mark 1983*. Necklace: 200 German 1-D-Mark coins,
weight 1 kg. Names of the models: Gabi and Robert. © Otto Künzli/VG Bild-Kunst

The Matter In Hand

Martina Margetts

Craft means creativity, activity and productivity. In contrast, the meaning of material is full of ambiguity. We live in a time when we cannot trust our perceptions about materials and a materialist world. *Swiss Gold*, Otto Künzli's seminal gold-bar brooch of 1983, is in fact just gold cardboard, a questioning of value(s) to prove the point. Today's internet deprives us of a connection with things: obsessed by surfing images, we consume superficially and judge prejudicially. This essay proposes that practices engaged with tangible materiality – through the lens of the elemental, desirable, ephemeral and sustainable – illuminate our current human existence. The essay does not discount aesthetics: on the contrary, it is through the aesthetics of material that ethics and politics come to light.

Elemental

Two theoretical propositions inform this section. My first is that nature's elemental materiality – earth, fire, water, air – combines durability with inherent flux, a combination which also characterises the human condition. A passage in *Thought Styles* by the anthropologist Mary Douglas discusses 'four distinctive myths of nature', as defined by the sociologist Michael Thompson. These are that 'nature is robust', 'nature is unpredictable', 'nature is robust but only within limits' and 'nature is fragile and pollution can be lethal'.[1] Different types of human behavioural attitudes are attached to these differing views of nature, respectively that of development entrepreneurs, non-committal fatalists, controlling planners and green lobbyists. Douglas concludes, 'The task of cultural theory is to show how...each vision of nature derives from a distinctive vision of society'.[2] It is only

---

1   Mary Douglas, *Thought Styles: Critical Essays on Good Taste* (London: Sage, 1994), 87. Michael Thompson's theory originated in M. Thompson, R. Ellis, A. Wildavsky, *Cultural Theory* (Boulder, CO: Westview Press, 1990).

2   Ibid., 90.

by reconciling, rather than reinforcing, differences that the task of environmental well-being, and with it human well-being, can be secured. Thus, the material resource of nature is both a cultural and a socio-political matter.

My second proposition is that the human body is active matter. Like the universe, the body is not a passive receptacle, for it expresses a continuously evolving experience of existence, which is embedded in its matter. However, in *The Body in Society*, sociologist Alexandra Howson spotlights our lack of body consciousness in everyday life: 'First, mind and body are considered distinct from each other and, second, body is subordinate to mind, where the former resembles a machine or an object in which the self is located. Third, the mind is considered the source of thought through which the self is produced.'[3]

Given this apprehension in today's world of the body as detached from generating thought, the body – human matter with somatic resonance – has not been sufficiently recognized as a locus of insight, creativity and meaning. Maurice Merleau-Ponty's book *Phenomenology of Perception* (1945) perceives that the active body 'positions its world around itself', for it is through the body that we experience the world. In a firm rejection of Descartes' mind/body dualism, Merleau-Ponty believes meaning is produced by 'an engaged body-subject'.[4]

Thus, both the natural world and the human body constitute what I would call 'thinking matter'. Earth, fire, water and air are the first elements of material making and benchmark the flux of order and disorder prevalent in humans and in everyday life. These observations on nature/human/body relations can be applied to the exemplars of material practice which follow. In considering the elemental facet of these works, the conjunction between the material of place, object and human body intensifies their impact.

In Vienna in the winter of 2016, the ceramicist Edmund de Waal curated *During the Night* at the Kunsthistorisches Museum. His aim was to explore the universality of human anxieties and nightmares

---

3 Alexandra Howson, *The Body in Society: An Introduction* (Cambridge, UK: Polity Press, 2004), 3.

4 Maurice Merleau-Ponty, in Jane Collins and Andrew Nisbet, *Theatre and Performance Design: A Reader in Scenography* (London: Routledge, 2012), 235.

– the dark, unconscious and subconscious workings of our being.[5] He was inspired by an Albrecht Dürer watercolour (*Dream Vision; A Nightmare*, 1525), in which a cloud-form incubus dominates the centre of the composition. Across the centuries, choosing from the museum's collection of 7,000 objects, de Waal pinned down his neurosis through material exegesis: skins, insect and animal forms, huge and tiny monsters, grotesques and exquisite corals and amulets conveyed to the viewer a unifying vision of being alive but full of dread. For the visitor, calm and alarm were simultaneous: confronting the material evidence in the shadowy half-light, the particular materials touched the unconscious viscerally. De Waal's own contribution, *In the Night*, was one of his now familiar large-scale vitrine installations of numerous dark pots arranged like concrete poetry or musical notes on a stave. The pots were spaced apparently atonally, yet were unified by black, charcoal and grey glazes, some matt, some shiny, with the total effect of swimming into consciousness rather than into view, a phenomenological rather than an optical apprehension. Whilst his works are often viewed as material minimalism – Modernist in their apparent rational simplicity – *In the Night* reveals itself as contingent, ambivalent, its restless agitation of surface, of composition, and inflected, hand-formed porcelain creating a dialogue across the centuries of objects which suspend, rather than fix, time.

A few months later, Loris Gréaud opened his Glasstress commission in a vast disused glassblowing workshop in Murano.[6] Entitled *The Uplayed Notes Factory*, hundreds of irregular glass baubles, handblown in Murano, were hoisted to the ceiling, with fire erupting from a furnace at the back. Gradually the heat burst the outsize baubles, which cracked and crashed to the ground. The experience offered a cacophony of sound, conforming to Baudrillard's simulacra – a representation of a reality – in this case like an erupting earthquake, a ceiling on fire, a war zone. As Baudrillard noted in his thoughts about glass in *The System of Objects*, its modern appearance is overlooked in its reliable ubiquity, its solidity and its perfection. It forms the boundaries of everyday

5 *During the Night*, curated by Edmund de Waal, Kunsthistorisches Museum, Vienna 10 October 2016 – 29 January 2017.

6 *The Unplayed Notes Factory,* by Loris Gréaud, curated by Nicolas Bourriaud, a Glasstress project for the 57th Venice Biennale in the disused Campollieto della Pescheria glass furnace, Murano 13 May – 26 November 2017.

life through which we casually see and touch, but both literally and metaphorically leaves us cold because of its familiarity. Gréaud's creation is the opposite: we stand safely back and dare not touch, viewers anxious and awed by the sublime. Like de Waal's project in Vienna, *The Unplayed Notes Factory* creates a state of flux: its sheer unfamiliarity and fragile, fiery materiality conjures eerie recollections of everyday life's explosive rhetoric during war promoted by the military-industrial complex. Who can forget the 2002 speech by Donald Rumsfeld seeking to justify the war in Iraq: 'There are known knowns. These are things we know that we know. There are known unknowns. That is to say, there are things that we know we don't know. But there are also unknown unknowns. There are things we don't know we don't know.' [7]

From the thick dark air of night and fire to earth: placing the natural body in an unnatural situation, Neil Brownsword's experimental *Marl Hole* project of 2009 tested the primordial relationship to material in a project beyond the confines of gallery spaces. [8] He was joined by three renowned fellow ceramicists from Scandinavia – Torbjørn Kvasbo, Alexandra Engelfriet and Pekka Paikkari – at Gorsty Quarry near Ibstock, whose clay supplies the largest brickworks in the UK. For five days, they could occupy the space and the material, in all types of weather, so that they experienced the exhaustion of labour and the primeval embodiment of clay as a creative inspiration rather than as dirt, which in Mary Douglas's view 'offends against order'. [9] In a reversal of all forms of sequential, ordered mastery, the ceramicists were dis-placing themselves in an encounter where control could not be expected: they had to submit to the elemental material. Perhaps Engelfriet's experience, recorded in the *Marl Hole* film, reveals the most explicit definition of 'truth to material', played out well beyond

---

7   12 February 2002, US Department of Defense transcript: http://archive.defense.gov/Transcripts/Transcript.aspx?TranscriptID=2636 (accessed 16 January 2018). The words by Donald Rumsfeld, then US Secretary of State for Defense, were part of his response to a question at a news briefing about the lack of evidence linking the government of Iraq with the supply of weapons of mass destruction to terrorist groups.

8   *Marl Hole* project, August 2009, originated by Neil Brownsword, film by Johnny Magee on Vimeo: https://vimeo.com/53679429 (accessed 16 January 2018).

9   Mary Douglas, *Purity and Danger: An Analysis of the Concepts of Pollution and Taboo* (London: Routledge classics, 1966), 2.

Kate MccGwire: *Evacuate*, 2010. Mixed media installation with game feathers.
Photo: Jonty Wilde

the expectation of William Morris or Bernard Leach, whose domestic circumscription of their material could not offer a direct impression of the human soul-charged body, as does her immersive imprint on the earth. There is instability, at once an ecstatic and abject state, akin to works by Cuban American Ana Mendieta, and embodied thought, which oblige us to expand the parameters and implications of our definition of contemporary materialism.

One could summarise *Marl Hole* as symbolic of Dionysian disorder and passion, wrestling with a search for origins. The opposite elemental material is mirrored glass, deployed with Apollonian eloquence in the work of American glass artist Josiah McElheny.[10] In the 'mirror phase', psychoanalyst Jacques Lacan credits the infant child with coming to terms with its environment and human relationships through the gaze, looking at its parent and looking anew through a mirror.[11] The apprehension of the world *as we perceive it* is an aesthetic, social and political act. McElheny's works invite us to transcend the inclination only to see what we want to see. His installations of blown and moulded glass vessels, of mirrored vitrines of 'goods' presented in illusionistic dialogue with the viewer to both confound and induce wonder and disorientation – in bright light not de Waal's penumbra – provide a feeling for the alienation of modern life through its pristine condition of material surface and volume in a white cube space. Elsewhere, McElheny fuses his interests in science and cosmology with glittering and sparkling giant crystalline clusters, like galaxies in space. In a recent performed installation, dancers wear mirrored placards provoking visitors to confront their self-regard. The dazzling play of light and refraction, of movement created by the multiple mirrored images and by us as viewers, embeds experience in us. Through sense perception, the material shapes our experience *from within* as well as optically.

10 Josiah McElheny: *Crystal Landscape Painting*, 2017. *Interactions of the Abstract Body*, 2012. *Island Universe*, 2008: http://whitecube.com/artists/josiah_mcelheny/ Also *Endlessly Repeating Twentieth Century Modernism*, 2007: http://www.andrearosengallery.com/artists/josiah-mcelheny/images (accessed 16 January 2018).

11 Jacques Lacan, 'The Mirror Stage as Formative of the Function of the I as Revealed in Psychoanalytic Experience', 1949, in *Ecrits, A Selection*, translated by Alan Sheridan (London: Tavistock Pulbications, 1977), 502–509: 502, 503.

Italo Calvino's essay on 'Lightness' poetically and eruditely explores the appeal of conditions which are the opposite of weighty.[12] In a representation of 'lightness' using water and air, the jeweller David Roux-Fouillet's necklace is a construct of linked metal 3D diamond-shaped outlines, which are passed through a container of soap-bubble water: the viscous water fills each link to create a glistening 'diamond' necklace. The lightness of the conceit is entirely in the spirit of Calvino's discourse, which unites the arts and sciences, the Classical mythic and our modern world by giving attention to material culture. The magical quality of Roux-Fouillet's necklace ushers us towards the realm of desire.

Desirable

'Wishes are memories coming from our future!' is how the German poet Rainer Maria Rilke encapsulates the out-of-reach longing that partly defines desire.[13] As a result, desire, which is at once conscious and sub-conscious, induces pleasure and anxiety, attraction and the fear of its implications. Seductive materialism can be exemplified by a quartet of objects across a century of time. First, Otto Künzli's brooch, mentioned at the start of the essay, because, as Annelies Moors explains, gold is a material asset, a 'supercurrency' whereby the wearing of gold jewellery 'then connects what is often seen as separate: the monetary system and notions of personhood, economy and emotions, investments and adornments'.[14] Second, Duchamp's *Fountain*, which metamorphoses the daily base function of the shiny white-glazed urinal into a metaphor of erotic and relational discourse simply by its relocation into an art gallery in 1917. Third, Meret Oppenheim's fur-covered cup, saucer and spoon (*Fur Breakfast,* 1936), which the Surrealism scholar Dawn Ades describes as 'function denied, the suffocatingly sensuous softness of fur displaced from touch to taste... the fetishistic character of many Surrealist objects...which play with erotically

12 Italo Calvino, *Six Memos for the Next Millennium* (New York: Vintage International, 1996), 3–29.
13 Rainer Maria Rilke, *Letters on Life,* ed., translated and introduced by Ulrich Baer (London: Modern Library Classics, 2006).
14 Annelies Moors, 'Wearing Gold', *Border Fetishisms: Material Objects in Unstable Spaces,* ed. Patricia Spyer (London: Routledge, 2009), 208-223:2.

charged substitutions for fragments of the body',[15] and fourth, Ted Noten's transparent acrylic handbag with an embedded gold-plated gun (*Lady K,* 2004).

Noten satirises capitalist societies which make a fetish of consumption, fomenting desire for everyday functional objects, such as a handbag, which is somehow imbued with mythic emotional power. A handbag's buckles, punched holes, handles, flaps, stitching, pockets, zips, studs and leathers orchestrate an intense excess of materiality and labour which act as a metaphor for emotional layers of want in a ritual object. Materialism alerts us to desire, ambivalence and possible disgust. In a discourse on the fetish, Peter Pels explains its ambivalent bridging between the allure of commercial goods and the inexplicably monstrous, which I will allude to shortly in the work of Kate MccGwire. Pels writes: 'The fetish foregrounds materiality because it is the most aggressive expression of the social life of things... Fetishism is animism with a vengeance. Its matter strikes back.' He further perceives that: 'On the one hand, the fetish is a material presence that does not represent but "takes one's fancy", making us suffer sensuously. On the other, it is only fanciful to us because it reminds us of a displacement and signals a loss or denial.'[16]

Kate MccGwire's alienating environments maximise these emotions: huge feathered anthropomorphic headless torsos are suspended like corpses, or reptilian monster forms writhe across floors and ooze out of fireplaces and drainpipes, so that the visitor to a kitchen or sitting-room is transfixed by what Freud calls the *unheimlich* – the unfamiliar, unappealing and repressed. Freud is attracted by Schelling's perception that 'everything is *unheimlich* that ought to have remained secret and hidden but has come to light'.[17] In *Border Fetishisms*, Michael Taussig further elucidates the emotional complexity with a comment on 'withinness', as being 'more than a fact of space or of autonomy, but a fact of metaphysics, religion and ontology... the

---

15 Dawn Ades, exhibition essay, *'Cosy: Freddie Robins'* (Colchester: Firstsite, 2002).

16 Peter Pels, 'The Spirit of Matter: on Fetish, Rarity, Fact and Fancy', *Border Fetishisms: Material Objects in Unstable Spaces*, ed. Patricia Spyer (London: Routledge, 2009), 91–121: 91, 114.

17 Sigmund Freud, 'The Uncanny', in *Writings on Art and Literature* (Redwood City, CA: Standord University Press, 1997), 193–234: 200.

connection of "innerness" to both the fetish power of the secret and animality'.[18]

Such emotions embedded in materiality were critiqued in Adolf Loos's seminal polemic already a century ago, when in Vienna his search for a rational modernity led him to write *Ornament and Crime* in 1908.[19] In coruscating prose, Loos remonstrated against decorative arts and intensive skilled labour as wasteful of material and human resources and a capitulation to a primitive age of bodily attention. In his view, nature, emotion and artistic form all needed to be brought under control. Loos sought a decorum of material presence with appropriate emotional and sensory restraint.

A century later, in 2007, Geoffrey Mann re-configured his knowledge of ceramic material to offer a brilliant contemporary riposte to Loos's strictures. He created a set of bone-china tableware, the forms of which were digitally produced following the sound-wave recording of the bitter marital argument acted out by Kevin Spacey and Annette Bening in the film *American Beauty*.[20] It is epitomised by the husband's lament: 'Our marriage is just for show. A commercial for how normal we are when we're anything but.' Beyond seeing the two actors at the table, we, as users, can experience, through direct touch, the tea-service deformed by their argument. The *dys*function is evoked by the material's mimetic qualities: bulges, ripples and curves appear in the wrong places like a parody of normal tableware – misshapen everyday things for misshapen lives. These are objects which literally embody the disruptive excesses of human behaviour.

18 Michael Taussig, 'Crossing the Face', *Border Fetishisms: Material Objects in Unstable Spaces*, ed. Patricia Spyer (London: Routledge, 2009). 228.

19 Adolf Loos, *Ornament and Crime*, reprinted in *The Architecture of Adolf Loos: An Arts Council Exhibition* (London: Arts Council of Great Britain, 1985, first published in 1908), 100–103.

20 *American Beauty*, directed by Sam Mendes, written by Alan Ball, Dream Works Pictures, 1999. Geoffrey Mann, *Cross-Fire, Natural Occurrence* series, 2010, computer-aided design, rapid prototyping, slipcast bone china: http://onviewonline.craftscouncil.org.uk/4040/object/P494 Film of *Cross-Fire* directed by Geoffrey Mann: https://vimeo.com/9256428 (accessed 16 January 2018).

Phoebe Cummings: *Anetdiluvean Swag*, 1.6 m wide, handbuilt, unfired clay, site-specific, New Art Centre, England 2016. Photo: Sylvain Deleu.

Ephemeral

Geoffrey Mann pinpoints the breakdown of desire through the application of sound waves to ceramic material. We may hang on to material or we may let go – as a demonstration of individual presence in the world, of a relationship with memory and to other people. I propose that those who work creatively to foreground the operation of material in ephemeral ways are engaged in a form of *resistance*. Material is invested with comments on values. To consider this, two projects, which allowed for interaction by visitors across a terrain of possessions, represent polar opposites of human experience. Michael Landy's *Break Down*, 2001, was a gigantic conveyor-belt installation designed to shred everything he had ever possessed, numbering 7,227 things, from his car, clothes and childhood toys to his friends' art, which included works by Damien Hirst and Tracey Emin.[21] The venue was an empty department store on Oxford Street, London's most famous shopping street, to highlight the paradox that in this space, goods were not for sale but for systematic destruction. The act of shredding his material goods also involved shredding money. The specificity of the vast array of materials passing before the visitors' gaze heightened the hopelessly ambivalent condition of every participant: the viewers, the artist, the possessions, the conveyor-belt workers, the disposal unit, the health and safety executives, the landfill agents. The supposed care which everyone had for each other and for the environment was upended.

This perverse creativity over ten days on a haunting production line 'manufactured' an erasure of selfhood, identification and object relations. Song Dong's *Waste Not* did the opposite: the Chinese artist set out to display everything Zhao Xiangyuan, his mother, had ever possessed – 10,000 things in regimented rows: used plastic food containers, toothpaste tubes, socks, blankets, cookware, furniture and so on, hoarded over five decades by his mother who had experienced personal grief and anxious deprivation during the years of the Cultural Revolution in China.[22] In both narrative projects, the vast array of materials provide a specific lexicon of touched memories, engendering

---

21 Michael Landy, *Break Down*, Oxford Street, London 10 February – 24 February 2001, an Artangel project: https://www.artangel.org.uk/project/break-down/ (accessed 16 January 2018).

22 *Song Dong: Waste Not*, The Curve Gallery, Barbican Centre, London 15 February – 12 June 2012.

empathy in the viewer. The ephemerality of everyday life is marked out by possessions in a relation to the body. In the drama of the different conditions of material possessions in time and space, viewers can acknowledge the possibility of renewal after loss.

A resistance to a status quo: for Landy, the insistence that things should be forgotten; for Song Dong that things should be remembered. Zhang Huang fuses the two – remembering and forgetting – in self-portraiture. He uses his own face as a surface for inscribing words in inked Chinese script. He does this to narrate the fate of his family. In *Family Tree*, 2001, which consists of nine large chromogenic photographs, each 53 × 41 cm, he starts with a handful of markings and gradually progresses to an entirely black-inked face where words can no longer convey meaning, where utterance fails. It is an astonishing evocation, with wider socio-political intent, a poignant self-mutilation to show a personal and collective suffering and loss of identity because the face literally fades to black.[23]

Ephemerality can be experienced in colour and sound through digital manipulation – examples being Richard Vijgen's tapestry, in which thermochromic yarn visualises Wi-Fi signals emitted by smart devices in a range of changing colours, and Imogen Heap's electronic gloves, which when animated by the hands, create soundwaves and can create music. Phoebe Cummings alerts us to the temporality of nature in the most poetic realization of raw material:[24] clay dug from the earth, worked by hand over several weeks into exquisite Baroque still lives of flowers, rocks, trees, fauna, sometimes whole room-sized landscapes, then left in this raw state to gradually decompose, symbolic of the fragility of nature and our existence. The choice of material is crucial to her purpose, for it is raw clay from which it is mythically asserted that God created man, a fusion of nature and culture at its origin. She makes the material convey its ultimate meaning: dust to dust. The ephemerality inherent in the process of making further alerts the viewer to the contemplation of time passing and the ethics

23 *Family Tree* by Zhang Huang, set of nine chromogenic prints, each 53 × 41 cm, 2001. Collection: Yale University Art Gallery. See *Between Past and Future: New Photography and Video from China* (London: Victoria and Albert Museum, 2005), 140.

24 Phoebe Cummings is the winner of the inaugural £10,000 BBC Woman's Hour Craft Prize, December 2017.

Lee Mingwei: *The Mending Project*, 2009/2017. Mixed media interactive installation. Installation view at the 57th International Art Exhibition – La Biennale di Venezia 'Viva Arte Viva', curated by Christine Macel. Photo: Anpis Wang

of production. For whilst Cummings resists the culture of museology, whereby things are collected over time to order our understanding of civilization, she wistfully acknowledges that her works will never stand the test of time and be able to be markers of her own time. The question is raised: What is sustained through material?

Sustainable

Underlying the four facets of this essay – elemental, desirable, ephemeral, sustainable – are forms of appraisal of material practice: aesthetic, ethical, cultural, socio-political. In this final section I juxtapose the sensors and the sensory. In the realm of *sensors* – chips, data, artificial intelligence, robotics – lies the technological challenge to our human materiality and soul: are *we* sustainable? In the realm of the *sensory* lies a concept of collective recuperation, repair and reconciliation, as a metaphor for what we value and wish to sustain.

The chips in smartphones have ushered in a different dialogue with material that has far-reaching implications for our societies, cultures, economies and politics. In the *Power of Making* exhibition at the V&A Museum in London in 2011, visitors who photographed a dress by Thorunn Arnadottir on their smartphone found that the crystal beaded patterning contained graphic codes which a mobile app could convert into text, images and links to websites. In a new form of interaction and object relation, visitors superseded merely envisioning wearing the dress, but literally communicated with it via the material. The materiality of goods has also been transformed, as media academics Graham Meikle and Mercedes Bunz explore in their new book *The Internet of Things*, which analyses this transformation of material understanding through technology:

> Things, from your phone to your car, from the heating to the lights in your house – have gathered the ability to sense their environments and create information about what is happening. Things have become media, able both to generate and communicate information.[25]

---

25 Mercedes Bunz and Graham Meikle, *The Internet of Things (Digital Media and Society)* (Cambridge, UK: Polity Press, 2017). Meikle's comment were noted at their seminar, University of Westminster, 22 November 2017.

There is a further evolution: Barbara Kruger's iconic collages a generation earlier, with slogans such as 'I shop therefore I am', would today read 'I am, therefore I am commodified': we ourselves are becoming the material in the form of data, we are the commodity which is being traded. Data is the new material and data is made of *us*, our private interests, tastes, choices, daily travels and our relationships, all recorded and capitalized on by Apple, Google, Amazon, Facebook and Microsoft.

While we as human beings are now the commodity, traded for commercial profit – natural material turned into data material – our memories are also being erased, by co-dependency on the internet, mobile phones and computer which store everything for us. Our individualism has been compromised. An essay by Katherine Viner summarises what is at stake:

> It is easy to feel that humanity is facing a great shift, about which we were not consulted. Overwhelming technological, environmental, political and social change has precipitated what the philosopher Timothy Morton memorably describes as 'a traumatic loss of co-ordinates' for all of us. What is becoming clear is that the way things have been run is unsustainable.[26]

Resistance to this human disorientation in relation to the internet lies in tangible craft: we can disarm the *sensors* with the *sensory*. It is a way of literally keeping in touch with things whilst maintaining equilibrium in the Anthropocene era. All over the world, creative practitioners are thinking this through in acts of material and social recuperation and repair. The Campana Brothers in Brazil recycle indigenous materials in their furniture and celebrate the folk traditions of the north-east; the Dutch duo Formafantasma's latest project *Ore Streams* recycles precious electronic metal waste;[27] Taiwanese Lee Mingwei's interactive clothes-repair project reminds us of the wastefulness of

---

26 Katherine Viner, *The Guardian*, 16 November 2017. Timothy Morton's quotation from an interview by Alex Blasden, 'A Reckoning for our Species: The Philosopher Prophet of the Anthropocene', *The Guardian*, 15 June 2017.

27 Formafantasma *Ore Streams* in NGV Triennial, National Gallery of Victoria, Melbourne, Australia, 15 December 2017 – 15 April 2018.

mass production,[28] while Julia Lohmann's lights made from seaweed and sheep's stomachs and Marlene Huissoud's household goods made from beehives and silk cocoons in the UK re-connect us to nature. Olafur Eliasson's *Green Light Project* brings together refugees, asylum seekers, migrants and NGOs (non-governmental agencies) to make lamps from recycled materials fitted with a green light. It is symbolic of the refugee condition that these production workshops are nomadic and have been held in Vienna, Houston and Venice since 2016.[29]

The four conceptions of nature outlined at the start of this essay serve to represent the attitudes which divide communities by hierarchies and apparent economic imperatives – or bring them together. Whilst this essay casts light on materiality through exhibitions and museum practices, it has also located meaning in other public places, in landscapes, shops and on the street. But perhaps it is the 'craftivists' and 'hackivists' who should have the last word, because their origins lie in a dialectical position, just like that of the critic.

Craftivism, like craft traditionally, is 'a way of thinking and acting upon the world as a means of self-development, critical reflection, education and making culture'.[30] Hackivists, according to Otto von Busch, pursue 'strategies of activism and critique' in relation to 'computer network technologies'. The craftivists and the hackivists are therefore respectively active in the arenas of what I call the sensory and the sensors 'in order to sustain an open source democracy in our global consumer society'.[31] Sustainability is rooted in collective intention. Their work and Eliasson's project relate to other materializations: the Maker Movement, Etsy, and communal bondings, such as those created by Lucy Orta and *Happy Campers* by WWIFM, whereby material costumes literally bound people together in street projects to express an avowal of socially diverse solidarity; 'civil disobedience workshops' for protest clothes promoted by Prêt-à-Révolter, and the Canadian Revolutionary Knitting Circle, whose

---

28 Lee Mingwei, *The Mending Project* 2009–2017 in *Viva Arte Viva*, Arsenale, 57th Venice Biennale, observed by the author on 12 November 2017.

29 *Green Light Project* at the 57th Venice Biennale, observed by the author on 12 November 2017.

30 Mike Press in Otto Von Busch and Karl Palmas, *Abstract Hacktivism – The Making of a Hacker Culture* (OPENMUTE.org, 2006), 34.

31 Ibid., 10, 15.

slogan is 'Building community, and speeding forward the revolution, through knitting'.

Those who share their values can elect to follow them – with whatever materials they may choose. My material is words. Bruno Latour [32] offers an affirmative view of the role of the critic: 'The critic is not the one who debunks, but the one who assembles...the one who offers the participants arenas in which to gather', as I have done here. When von Busch and Palmas looked at the etymology of the word 'thing', they found it included the definition 'meeting, assembly' alongside 'act, deed, event, material, object, body' and 'entity, being, matter'. Thus, consideration of matter embraces the wider ethics and politics of the social life of things – and of us.

---

32   Ibid., 11, quoting Bruno Latour, *Critical Inquiry*, vol. 30, no. 2.

.

Espen Sommer Eide & Signe Lidén: *Altitude and History, trek and concert.*
Performed near Nikel, Russia, in *Dark Ecology Journey 3*, June 2016.
Photo: Dark Ecology/Sonic Acts

Paying Attention to Material Responses in Local Ecologies

Hilde Methi

We drove inland. I had located some reindeer herders who had started separating their animals, gathering them inside fences. They agreed that we could come and that the artist Raviv Ganchrow could collect materials. We passed through the rich river valley and, ascending the fells, came upon a perfect mountain-shaped rocky mass of white minerals standing out in the landscape. It seemed to reflect spiritual energy. It was September, on the outskirts of the Caledonian rocks of Scandinavia. Turning onto a bumpy road, we eventually reached our destination. A spiral of running reindeer appeared, cans of fuel, and men, women and youngsters focused on their tasks. There was a hanging carcass, some wooden structures and a few four-wheel all-terrain vehicles. We parked next to them. No one seemed to pay attention to the fact that we were there, so we went inside the fences. Raviv Ganchrow installed himself and grounded his recording equipment to the earth in the hope of capturing the sounds of the running hooved animals. He had just begun exploring infrasound.

In the Dark Ecology project,[1] a section of the European Arctic borderland became a zone in which to think and act along a trajectory of new artistic works presented on three Dark Ecology Journeys (DEJ). The DEJ travellers were artists, cultural producers and scientists who presented artworks, lectures and stories while walking with local experts between the towns of Kirkenes in Norway and Nikel in Russia.

---

1 The Dark Ecology project (www.darkecology.net/aboutorg), by Dutch Sonic Acts and the Norwegian curator Hilde Methi, commissioned 20 works by artists, musicians, designers and architects, which were presented during week-long bus journeys that crossed the Norwegian-Russian border area in October 2014, November 2015, and June 2016. The idea of turning the area into an 'artistic zone' responded to the actual border-citizen zone (extending 50 km on each side) that, since 2012, has allowed citizens to visit the other side of the border without a visa.

To experience the heavily polluted towns and tundra of the zone – this is especially so on the Russian side – was, for many of the DEJ travellers, to face otherness and darkness. The participants reacted differently: one could not eat, others became obsessed with documenting the polluted nature, or with photographing the sublime, destroyed landscape. Another group turned their attention to the human activity that went on simultaneously, such as people caring for their animals or beautifying demolished buildings with plants, or they listened to peoples' stories about their love for their 'suffering town'.[2] Many of the DEJ travellers returned to the zone, especially the artists who were producing works there, so they became more familiar with it.

The temporary site-responsive works that were performed or installed at different locations also responded to recent thinking on ecology. Timothy Morton,[3] from whom the project coordinators borrowed the term 'dark ecology', argues for the need to get rid of the idea of nature as separate from the human being in order to see ourselves as always already bound up in a dark mesh of ontological feedback. The 'nature/culture' split in the humanities that Morton insists on erasing, resonates in some respects with an indigenous worldview, more particularly, with the partly forgotten (local) memory of the human as being-a-part. A realization of the individual human being's incompleteness and the radical necessity of others diminishes the significance of the individual and gives objects the possibility to act in the world.

In thinking about artistic production in relation to ecology and ontology, I think about materiality, not in terms of using a material,

---

2   Quoted from Britt Kramvig and Berit Kristoffersen, The Journey of Darkness, 2014: http://www.darkecology.net/field-notes/the-journey-of-darkness (accessed 10 January 2017).

3   Morton argues that the problem of environmental thinking is the image of nature itself. Instead of trying to use an idea of nature to heal what society has damaged, Morton sets out a new form of ecological criticism: dark ecology. See Timothy Morton, *Ecology Without Nature: Rethinking Environmental Aesthetics* (Cambridge, MA: Harvard University Press, 2007) and *Dark Ecology: For a Logic of Future Coexistence* (New York: Columbia University Press, 2016). Morton adopts a New-materialist perspective on the conventional culture/nature dichotomy in order to liberate his and his readers' thinking from it. He wants to affirm the difference between nature and culture. In this way, it should be possible to see mankind and nature as two sides of the same issue, yet not as the same. Nature is part of the human being, and the human being is part of nature.

but by posing a question: What makes a material come to matter as a world-making process? This world-making, which has also been called 'worlding', circumvents forms of representation, depiction or the mirroring of the world. When a work of art makes a world, it does not inquire into how we can know something; rather, it interrogates what it itself is – its materials, components and the circumstances of its making. In this way, it invites us to ponder on what reality is.

Artistic productions, also novel formats for artistic presentation, can be considered 'thinking-being things' that cut into different worlds of matter and meaning. The arts have been important for Morton and other thinkers in the field of object-oriented-ontology, as they argue that what the world needs is not analysis and interpretation, but imagination. In the local culture from which my curatorial work is spawned (and in which it preferably operates), storytelling is a common way to create and spread knowledge, and opinions are often expressed through intimation, or through other more indirect forms of communication. These were all integral to my work as a curator for the Dark Ecology project. In this article, I think through three Dark Ecology works that I consider material-based and based on the same material, namely, sound. Each of them makes materiality matter but in different ways. After exploring them (in part), I present my responses and associative stories and ideas. What is at stake here are attentiveness, art as response, and the ability to respond to art and the environment – response-ability – through hearing, seeing and feeling, which are necessarily both mental and bodily in nature.

Long waves

Long-Wave Synthesis (2014), by Raviv Ganchrow,[4] concerned the materiality of sound and sound as phenomenon (rather than a representation) and space. Ganchrow's original idea was to build a land-art scale sound-wave field of transducers.[5] This would allow for the production of acoustic territories that linked back to the notion of the specific

---

4 For a full transcription of the lecture by Raviv Ganchrow, see 'On Long Wave Synthesis', in *The Geological Imagination*, eds. Arie Altena, Mirna Belina and Lucas van der Velden (Amsterdam: Sonic Acts Press, 2015), 179–297.

5 'A transducer is a device that converts energy from one form to another. Usually a transducer converts a signal in one form of energy to a signal in another' https://en.wikipedia.org/wiki/Transducer (accessed 5 December 2017).

landscape. The plan was to go down to around 4 Hz, in other words, to frequencies in a range of roughly 10 to 85 meters long. The initial impetus for *Long-Wave Synthesis* was a question about the perception of a landscape in relation to long-wave vibrations. From there, Granchrow developed the notion of an incredible, mostly inaudible (to the human ear), world of colossal acoustic waves.

At some freestanding concrete walls, called the *Splinthangar*, near Kirkenes Airport, the artist installed a prototype enabling the audience to get a sense of his research on infrasound.[6] Here he also gave a lecture presenting his findings. What he had found was that the length of the infrasonic waves was much, much longer than he had anticipated, and while the frequency band that the human organism is oriented towards is roughly at a scale that interacts with small- to medium-sized objects in our environment, the scale of infrasound interacts with the scale of the topography or even of the atmosphere itself. In other words, the landscape, the globe and its gaseous surroundings impart aspects of their properties to the propagating sound waves. If there is a bandwidth in which the Anthropocene registers, this would be it, as infrasound literally connects the solid earth to oceans and weather, as well as to modern industrial practices. If we consider these large-scale transformations in spectral terms, instead of thinking of them as chemical and mineral evidence, the environmental infrasound would exhibit an intermingling of large-scale human industrialized activity along with these other frequencies that relate to the earth and the atmosphere.

Examples of some of the diverse events that occupy infrasound are exploding meteors, collapsing arctic glaciers, volcanic eruptions and auroras. As for anthropogenic contributions to the infrasound spectrum, there are mine explosions propagating in the ground and the air, debris from outer space re-entering the earth's atmosphere (almost daily), aircraft sonic booms, nuclear testing and much more.

---

6   The prototype consisted of a rotary (fan) transducer producing forward and backwards air motion. The signal used was from the nearby infrasound sensor at Bardufoss, station number IS37, part of the CTBT (Comprehensive Nuclear-Test-Ban Treaty); Global network of infrasound sensors, operated by the International Monitoring System (IMS). The playback was a 24-hour recording of environmental infrasound from 12 September 2014. The playback was in real time on the pneumatic transducer, producing polyrhythmic patters.

Lions, wolves and particularly elephants use infrasound for communication and seem to be aware of this environmental characteristic. The human attention to large sound waves and their role in geo-physical perception extends far back in time, not least through listening to the running of hooved animals.

Ganchrow's lecture must have lasted about one hour. He ended it by showing that his research had led him to explore how infrasound crosses a threshold where it interfaces with weather through barometric pressure and becomes weather.

While on-site, the DEJ travellers and members of the local community who joined the audience listened to and felt the infrasound generated by the prototype. It made us aware of the acoustic properties of the land – the specifically transmissive properties of local materials and geo-activity. We learned that what we locals call 'reindeer lichen' provides a kind of anechoic layer on the ground that creates very specific outdoor acoustics: direct sound is accentuated and ground reflections are diminished. The lichens allowed us to hear very clearly the fine details in those clicks that came from the prototype.

Air and wind

Altitude and History (2016) by Signe Lidén and Espen Sommer Eide was conceived as an exploration into sounds, verticality, the human body, memory and the wind around Nikel in Russia. In an essay written in conjunction with the work, Eide describes how these elements came together in their research that would eventually take the form of a trek and a concert in the hills near Nikel. Upon reaching a plateau overlooking an endless forest, we would come across several instruments built by the artists. These would be played by either the wind or the artists. Some of us had read the essay to prepare for experiencing the work. The idea, according to the artists, was 'to build instruments that assist sounds to write themselves in the air'.[7]

To trace Nikel's audible past, Lidén and Eide initiated the 'Nikel Sound History Club' and reached out to elderly local residents who had lived in Nikel most of their lives. The artists asked the club members to remember sounds they used to hear in the area at certain times and

---

7   Quoted from Espen Sommer Eide, 'A Vertical Perspective', in *Living Earth: Field Notes from the Dark Ecology Project 2014–2016*, ed. Mirna Belina (Amsterdam: Sonic Acts Press, 2016), 165.

Margrethe Pettersen: *Living Land – Below as Above*. Sound-walk at the frozen lake Postmestervatn near Kirkenes, performed during *Dark Ecology Journey 2*, November 2015. Photo: Dark Ecology/Michael Miller

to try to put into words what they sounded like: '…old soundscapes of Nikel were brought into the present. The animal clamour from the collective farms, the sound of wood chopping in the apartments before lighting the morning stove, the screams of a non-human creature in the mine'.[8] All the stories inspired the building of a socio-technological, harmonica-like storytelling device. The artists used it to 'blow' the stories out of the instrument, some in Russian and some in English.[9]

The artists' longstanding interest in sound and memory was connected to the local context through the Nikel Sound History Club. This also became a bridge between the local community and those of us who were participants in DEJ. When we as group of artists and researchers were walking around with our cameras, sound recorders and local guides, we did not exactly blend into the environment (sometimes we walked around in snowmobile suits while our big yellow bus stood parked at Lenin Square). Children often stopped to practise their English skills on us. The clammy tourist-group feeling, especially during DEJ1 which Lidén and Eide attended, was reacted to and addressed through a more dialogical approach.

When *Altitude and History* was finally performed, an equal number of locals as DEJ participants showed up. Forming a group of about 100 people, we walked across sparsely vegetated, soft and toxic soil, up into the hills and with our backs to the chimneys of Nikel. Espen Sommer Eide stopped now and then to play their harmonica-like instrument: from it we heard a voice narrating 'Nikel's sound memories'. The second part of the event involved listening to the wind instruments that the artists had built and installed on a plateau overlooking the huge forest valleys surrounding the Nikel 'desert'. When we arrived at this site, the wind had stilled and the instruments did not make any sound. The artists, having to improvise, started to talk about the instruments and demonstrate how they worked. Some could be swung in a circle around the body, generating a surround-sound effect. Before the third and final part of the event – a wonderful concert by the two artists

---

8   Sommer Eide, *A Vertical Perspective*, 168.

9   The transcription of the stories and their narration was done by Maria Rusinovskaya, who was also a co-curator and producer of the work. Roman Khoroshilov, the local Dark Ecology coordinator, helped organize the meeting in Nikel Sound History Club and provided translation at the meeting.

for those of us attentive to it – the audience started to engage with the amplifiers on the ground. They took turns waving the 'surround instruments' and ran with them to get the sound effects. The artists were no longer in complete control, improvising in an unintentional collective situation. It was as if some kind of local radiation was affecting the encounters between all the components they brought together.

The audience became co-generators of various sounds in the air – the 'core carrier' of sound – along with the sulphur dioxide emissions from the factory chimneys of Nikel. It is these that Norwegian authorities have been unsuccessful in trying to get rid of through the last three decades. Making the wind an essential part of the work not only 'hit the nail on the head'; it also gave presence to the serious aspect of Dark Ecology.

Ice and snow

Living Land – Below as Above (2015), a sound walk by Margrethe Pettersen, was the enactment of the frozen landscape and the beings living on, in and below the land and ice. While listening to an audio piece through earphones, the participants walked a certain route on a frozen lake near Kirkenes. This work was commissioned for the Polar-Night edition of the DEJ, when snow enfolded the landscape and animals hibernated. The spectrum of what was visible and audible was scaled down and invited us to use our senses to pay closer attention to nuances. *Living Land – Below as Above* explored new ways to experience forms of life in a lake, underneath ice. It was narrated through living memories and local Sámi myths voiced by the artist and others.

A suggested route was torch lit. Human tracks were made in the snow. While walking, we spotted networks of tracks from different animals such as a fox, grouse and unidentified others. We did the sound walk in the dark on the horizontal layer of thin ice and witnessed the multiple others we live with and their worlds.

Through the DEJs, different assemblages of relations were enacted. While Margrethe Pettersen was producing her work, the anthropologist Britt Kramvig was doing research on Sámi *seidis*, or stones. She searched through archives to collect written records of seidi sites and the stories connected to them. Pettersen and Kramvig met on several occasions during the research period, mostly to explore vague ideas for a text they co-wrote and for the sound walk. From the start, the two read the same academic texts and old books with place-based

Exploring the old growth forest around Mustarinda.
Photo: Dan McCabe

Raviv Gaschrow: *Long Wave Synthesis*. Work in progress, lecture and
demonstration at Splinthangaren during Dark Ecology Journey 1, October 2014.
Photo: Dark Ecology/Konstantin Guz

Sámi storytelling events. They aired their ideas about the connection between past events and present socio-material stories of and on the land. This was a collaborative way of working and knowing.

Can we hear the stories told by other spirits living on the land? Can we hear the sound of the atmosphere and from within the ice? Questions such as these were the starting point for Margrethe Pettersen's work. Whilst walking, we heard, through earphones, sounds and stories told in voices speaking several languages. When nothing was being told, we heard our own footsteps in the snow.

> Sssssssssssssssssssuuuuuuuuouououoooossssssssssssssssssssssuuuuuuouoouou-ossuouuouosssuouossssssssssssssssssssssuuuuuuoooooossssssssssssssssss sssssuuuuuihhhiihiiuuuussssss

> I am snow – *muhottit* – I take many forms – dry and light, wet and heavy, crisp and hard, calm or whipping. Like a silent carpet I cover everything. Hopefully I calm you down. I give brightness in a period when everything is dark and give shelter if you form me properly.

Multiple voices came from different positions, for instance: 'I am snow' and 'I am a water plant'. The voices did not necessarily speak for the snow or the water plant but showed the importance of listening to them. Pettersen and Kramvig were inspired by the anthropologist Marisol De la Cadena's concept of 'anthropo-not-seen', which refers to the particles of the world that are often not seen, including the assemblage of human and non-human particles. It could also be translated as 'articulated collectives' of nature and humans.[10]

Response-ability

To recall sound is to activate memories 'unhinged from chronological time'.[11] Materials store and carry memories. 'Hearing is a way of touching the weather. What does it mean to be present in a place, to sit still and listen to faraway cries of dogs and shouts of children carried by the wind? Even when we do not want to remember, our memories wash over us, uninvited.'[12]

---

10 Britt Kramvig and Margrethe Pettersen, 'Living Land – Below as Above', in *Living Earth,* 130ff.
11 Sommer Eide, A Vertical Perspective, in *Living Earth*, 174.
12 Sommer Eide, A Vertical Perspective, in *Living Earth*, 168.

Air carries the sound that we humans are used to hearing. Sound is physical when the air pressure of molecules hits hair cells inside our ears. Animals use sound, as for instance infrasound in relation to navigation. Sound propagates in water and in solid materials. Infrasound consists of long waves that travel on a planetary scale. We humans usually do not hear infrasound, but we can sometimes feel its waves if we are attentive to the ground. 'Within vibrations themselves, there are no abrupt boundaries, no distinctive thresholds, only heterogeneous continuities afloat on a flux of becoming', writes Raviv Granchrow.[13]

The composer and music theorist John Cage once said that when composers started to engage with sound as a material and a phenomenon, it was with the realization that we as humans are not separate from nature. Sound is omnipresent and silence does not exist: we are 'technologically equipped to transform our contemporary awareness of nature's manner of operation into art (...) and let sounds be themselves rather than (...) expressions of human sentiments (...). The opposite is what is meant by response ability'.[14]

Response-ability means that humans and non-humans get involved in each other's projects and co-existence. The eminent scholar Donna Haraway calls this 'becoming-with' the entity in question. Projects enacting multiple worlding are projects committed to 'becoming involved in one another's lives'.[15] Response-ability is the possibility to respond to something, whether it be human, another form of life or something non-animate, as for instance a story or worlding project. In *Altitude and History,* the wind made itself matter because of its absence.

In *Living Land – Below as Above,* the local, indigenous land with its attendant forms of life was enacted (represented), whereas the undomesticated moments (of silence) made us attentive to the index of the sosio-material world. In *Long-Wave Synthesis,* we were given opportunities to reflect on the long sound waves propagating throughout the earth and the atmosphere. In these presentations, we were able to

---

13 Raviv Ganchrow, 'Hear and There: Notes on the Materiality of Sound' in *Oase # 78. Immersed. Sound and Architecture*, eds. Paulina Avidar, Raviv Ganchrow and Julia Kursell (Rotterdam: NAi Publishers), 78.

14 John Cage, *Silence*, (Middletown, CT: Wesleyan University Press, 1961), 9–10.

15 Donna Haraway, *Staying with the Trouble: Making Kin in the Chthulucene* (Durham, NC and London: Duke University Press, 2016), 71.

study the technological generating object – whether it was a prototype, an instrument or an amplifying unit built by the artist – but we could also experience and study the way in which the object responded to its surroundings and to our bodies.

Low-frequencies and the local scale

In Raviv Ganchrow's demonstration, the local environment came to the fore as vibration. I was excited to learn that what we call 'reindeer lichen' helped us hear the clicks of the amplified infrasound. Lichens and corals are examples of symbiotic living: they are combinations of fungus and algae. The algae part does the photosynthesis that the fungus part cannot do, and the two parts help each other with food exchange (exactly how it happens is still a mystery to biologists). Lichens are small and beautiful and grow about one centimetre in ten years. They are the corals of the land. The North-Sami word for lichen, *jeagil*, has been adapted to the Russian language as *jagl*, 'jágel'. The little language gave one word to the big language. I also started to think about the type of traditional Sámi song called *yoik* in relation to infrasound, as yoik is non-representational. In yoik, a person does not sing *about* something; rather, the person yoiks something or someone. Yoik involves lower frequencies of the voice register that affect the body differently than do the frequencies of the upper register. Perhaps yoik in its low frequencies could be considered the infrasound of the body.

And perhaps *duodji*, traditional Sami handicraft of various kinds, or part of it, is also low-frequency, as it involves on-going, long-term transformative material processes that demand a sensitivity to non-human beings. Embedded in the word doudji, which is also a verb, is the notion of attentiveness to spiritual material in the making. For some duodji works made of wood, the transformation process continues after the artist has finished them, as they are placed in nature to decompose.[16] In both yoik and duodji, there are traces of humble making, and since neither yoik nor duodji are built on the 'idea of the author', they would be considered largely co-worked material forms of making (co-worked with the material, or, as in the case of yoik, with the one is yoiking). Both duodji and yoik require material access, but like a bass-drum, they could be placed anywhere in a room and still be sensed.

---

16 Examples are works by the late dujar and artist Iver Jåkes.

Mustarinda and the Rural Reading Room

I am writing this in Mustarida, in the mid-eastern part of Finland, in an old-growth forest bordering on Russian Karelia. It is here that artists, activists and scientists have been voluntarily running a residency and an exhibition space for about ten years. They are staying with the forest. It is a story of hope.[17] I am here with Kristin, a colleague from the 'Rural Reading Room'.[18] Kristin and I will continue to work on 'local text' here where everything points to nature and energy. We are participating in a thematic residency programme called 'post-fossil aesthetics'. The house gets its heat and electricity for most of the year from a geothermal system run by a do-it-yourself compost-container and solar panels, even though this is in the snowiest part of wintery Finland. Yesterday morning, one of us climbed up on the roof to shovel the snow off the solar panels. We got enough electricity to heat the electrical sauna in the afternoon.

On a walk in the forest with Nyyska, a local resident who is part of the Mustarinda association, we of course ask: 'How old is the spruce?' A spruce tree has a one-thousand-year cycle, she says. One should not think of a tree as a single individual that stands or 'lives' for 300 years, but as part of a system. This old-growth forest has never been clear-cut. It is 10,000 years old. A system for living and dying over such a long period has developed an ability to adapt to change – a much needed ability in a time of climate change. Nyyska talks about the many organisms that enjoy being here, including herself, often having what she calls 'a direct experience' while in the forest. I guess direct experience is a form of knowledge from a sensational-spiritual experience. It could be 'to become other'. In this area, and especially on the Russian side in Karelia, there are also traces of animism in cultural rituals. Mustarinda, which means black chest or breast, refers to the bear. Being here is transformative.

---

17 In the book *Staying with the Trouble*, Donna Haraway tells stories of becoming-with as stories of hope for how we can live and die well on a damaged planet.

18 The Rural Reading Room (organized by Espen Sommer Eide, Hilde Methi, Kristin Taarnesvik and Morten Torgersrud) tested out a format for art in peripheral places though one-week gatherings four times during the period 2013–2015.

Before the last gathering in the Rural Reading Room in 2015, some of us had been reading the book *Soul Hunters,* which tells about the hunter-gatherer culture of the Yukaghirs in Siberia.[19] The author introduces irony as an explanation for how the people practice their belief, in which for instance the bear is thought to be loaded with an unsurpassed potency of spirituality. When a bear is killed, the people follow a certain ritual with strict rules, which involves making the dead bear believe someone else has killed it (they do not call it a bear, but something akin to 'grandfather'). The author's point is that the jokes made around the ritual suggest that underlying the Yukaghir animistic cosmology, there is a force of laughter, of ironic distance, of making fun of the spirits. This does not mean that the Yukaghirs do not take the spirits seriously: they are a part of life, but they do not have lordship over life, as that would mean the spirits have a moral right to consume the Yukaghirs.[20]

What would an animistic or a mimetic response in the Rural Reading Room be like? We call out loud to each other in the forest, we walk extremely slowly, one of us mimics a salmon, we burn our table-top on a frozen lake, (this is dramatic, since the table-top used to be at the centre of our public presentations), we do a roundtable automatic speech session, from which we generate a poem. At the core of all this is a discussion on how we can approach a certain type of nature called *pals* (similar to what a pingo is in English), that is found in the swamps in the area. The four of us all agree that our first encounter with the pals was a bit too violent, since we had run around on it and put our table on it. Perhaps we had disgraced it. However, the person who wanted to show us the pals in the first place had brought along a lens, which

---

19 Rane Willerslev, *Soul Hunters: Hunting, Animism, and Personhood among the Siberian Yukaghir*, (Berkeley and Los Angeles: University of California Press, 2007).

20 To explain: a 'demand-sharing principle' regulates the relation between hunters and the spirits, meaning that the one party must always share with the other. The 'animal master spirit', which owns many animals, is morally obliged to give animals to the hunters, but during the actual hunt, the hunters will always be uncertain about whether there really is such an obligation. Hunters respond to this uncertainty by tricking the sprits to think that they themselves are not responsible for having hunted and killed animals. In this way, the risks that come with the demand-sharing principle and the giver-relation are minimized.

made a connection to the invisible 'lens' of underlying permafrost that maintains the pals. (When the permafrost melts the palses will disappear). We needed a second chance to encounter the pals.

Attention

What do the arts have to offer in the Anthropocene, Anthropo-not-seen, Anthropo-sceen, Capitolocene, Chthulucene, Antithropocene, Misantropocene period? At this moment, I would say that art, in its modest way, can draw sensible attention to something. Art has a job to do in engaging with other-then-human creatures of the Earth, but not necessarily by mimicking or representing 'the other'. Non-representational approaches that engage with ontology and materiality address first and foremost our perception, and through highlighting sensation, they can be instructive in a subtle way. Art can be experiential, sensational, or operational on-goingness, as a poetry of the practical, material and physical. Art demands active and attentive listening, smelling, reading or seeing, and through our senses, we can become-with one another. A motivating impetus behind a work is a response that generates a response. Art is a way of giving attention to and learning from our surroundings, together with others.

Here at Mustarinda we read aloud, we listen to each other reading from books, we share the experience of reading and listening, and we think together out loud. Two participants, Carina and Anna, once took us outside. As a group of nine gathered around the rain gutter at the corner of the house, we listened to the drops of water and an engine in the far distance as Carina and Anna read a poem they had written about water. Then they served us tea. The water droplets hit the ground with the pulse in our body. That was a moment of deep attention.

Rural Reading Room, Pals, 2015, documentation of a process, October 2015
Image: Rural Reading Room

Rural Reading Room, Building Double, documentation of a process,
November 2014

Contributors

EDITORS

Knut Astrup Bull is a senior curator at the National Museum of Art, Architecture and Design, Oslo. He has curated several contemporary craft exhibitions, including *Hverdagsliv – Everyday Life* (2007), *Tendencies 2010, Svein Thingnes: Ceramics 1970 – 2010* and *Needle's Eye: Contemporary Embroidery* (2015). He has authored the books *En ny diskurs for kunsthåndverket – en teori om det nye konseptuelle kunsthåndverket* (A New Discourse for Decorative Arts: A Theory of the New Conceptual Craft) (2007), and *Modus Operandi – Hensiktsmessighetens estetikk* (Modus Operandi: Aesthetics of Appropriateness) (2009) and co-edited and contributed to the book *Horizon: Transferware and Contemporary Ceramics* (2015).

André Gali is the head of critical theory and publications at Norwegian Crafts and series editor of *Documents on Contemporary Crafts*. He is also the founding editor of the Nordic art quarterly *Kunstforum* (acting as its editor up to 2015) and the website www.kunstforum.as, founded in 2009. He is currently also a senior advisor for the recently established Kunstforum Consulting. He holds a master's degree in theatre theory from the University of Oslo (2005). Gali has worked as a freelance art critic, photographer, essayist, journalist and lecturer, and has published essays on art and economy, queer and feminist art practices, the gaze of the middle class and on contemporary art jewellery. Selected catalogues and books are *Fornebu Art and Architecture Destination* (contributor/editor, 2017), *On Collecting* (contributor/editor, 2017), *Kampen med materialet – Norske Kunsthåndverkere i 40 år* (contributor/editor, 2015), *Crafting Exhibitions* (contributor/editor, 2015), *Aftermath of Art Jewellery* (contributor, 2013), *Morten Andenæs: Skyldfolk* (contributor, 2012), and *Never Mind the Benefits* (contributor, 2012).

Glenn Adamson is a curator, writer and historian who works across the fields of design, craft and contemporary art. He is currently a senior scholar at the Yale Center for British Art, and the editor-at-large of *The Magazine Antiques*. He has previously been the director of the Museum of Arts and Design (MAD) in New York, head of research at the Victoria and Albert Museum and a curator at the Chipstone Foundation in Milwaukee. Adamson's publications include *Art in the Making* (2016, co-authored with Julia Bryan Wilson), *Invention of Craft* (2013), *Postmodernism: Style and Subversion* (2011), *The Craft Reader* (2010), and *Thinking Through Craft* (2007). Most recently he was the co-curator of *Voulkos: The Breakthrough Years* at MAD (2016), curator of *Beazley Designs of the Year*, at the Design Museum in London (2017) and co-curator (with Martina Droth and Simon Olding) of *Things of Beauty Growing: British Studio Pottery*, at the Yale Center for British Art (2017).

Sarah R. Gilbert is an artist and educator based in Los Angeles. She is currently an assistant professor of sculpture at Pitzer College. Her work has been exhibited widely throughout the United States and internationally. Recent projects include *Goosebumps*, a participatory sound installation and satellite exhibition of the 2017 Applied Art Triennial: *Time Difference,* in Tallinn, Estonia, and *7 Barrios*, a community garden designed and built in collaboration with Valeria Florescano and the students and staff of Faro Tláhuac, in Mexico City, Mexico. Her current research explores intertwining natural history and material cultures of the late nineteenth and early twentieth century, in what is now called California.

Søren Kjørup's first writing on aesthetics was his introduction (1968) to the Danish translation of A.G. Baumgarten's Latin dissertation on poetry from 1735. His second publication, the textbook *Æstetiske problemer* (1971), presents his original version of the institutional theory of art. From 1973 to 2009 he was a professor of the history and theory of the humanities at Roskilde University. Since 2000 he has been developing a theory of the practice of artistic research. He was in the research group 'K-verdi' at Bergen National Academy of Art and Design from 2008 to 2011, acting as the theorist for the interdisciplinary project 'Art Value: A Research Project on Trash and Readymades, Art and Ceramics'.

Anders Ljungberg lives and works in Gustavberg, Sweden, but has exhibited, lectured and been a guest teacher many places in the world. A central theme in his artistic practice is the relationship between human beings, objects and space. He examines emotional, metaphorical and poetic understandings of everyday use. He is represented by Marzee in The Netherlands, Galerie Rosemarie Jäger in Germany and Konsthantverkarna in Stockholm. His works can be found in the collections of Marzee in Nijmegen, the National Museum in Stockholm, Röhsska in Gothenburg, the National Museum of Art, Architecture and Design in Oslo, the Nordiska Museum in Stockholm and the Royal Collection in Stockholm. Ljungberg received his training in art at Konstfack in Stockholm (1989–1994) and later became a senior lecturer at the school (2000–2010). He was for two years a professor at Oslo National Academy of the Arts, in the metal and jewellery department (2014–2016). Since 2016 he has been back in Stockholm, as professor for the study programme 'CRAFT!' at Konstfack.

Martina Margetts' nine years as editor of the British journal *Crafts* and her decades of postgraduate teaching at the Royal College of Art have enabled a continual testing of ideas about craft. Her focus is on contemporary practice in global socio-cultural frameworks. She teaches, writes, curates, broadcasts and lectures internationally, working with major national and international institutions. She is on the advisory board of the *Journal of Modern Craft* and the journal *Craft Research*. Her books include *International Crafts* (1991), *Michael Rowe* (2003) and *Tord Boontje* (2007). Most recently, she has contributed to *Contemporary Clay and Museum Culture* (2016) and *The Ceramics Reader* (2017). Exhibitions which she has curated include *The Raw and the Cooked: New Work in Clay in Britain* (1993, co-curated with Alison Britton), *Objects of Our Time* (1996/7), *Only Human* (1999/2000, for the Crafts Council), and *Time Machines: Daniel Weil and the Art of Design* (2014, for the Design Museum). A recent British-Council study visit to Thailand was the basis for her curation of *On the Line: New Perspectives on Craft in Southeast Asia* (2017, Aram Gallery, London).

Hilde Methi is a curator based in Kirkenes, Norway. Her work investigates the relation between her own local position and the larger geopolitical setting. She builds up long-term collaborative projects that introduce artistic ideas into the local context. She conceived the Sámi Art Festival, which was held in various places in the Barents Region and in Sápmi (2008–2011). Methi has co-curated *russianmarket.info – Taking Inventory*, Uqbar (2011), *YNKB*, Copenhagen (2011), *Extreme Crafts*, Freies Museum, Berlin (2012), the biennial *Nørrekærbiennalen* (2014), and co-founded the art collectives *Mobile Kultur Byrå* (2006– ongoing) and *Rural Reading Room* (2012–2015). She has just concluded the first series of 'Dark Ecology' projects in collaboration with Sonic Acts in the Netherlands. These three-year projects include temporary installations, audio-visual performances and sound-walks in the border zone between Northern Norway and Russia. Methi is currently also curating at Ä'vv Skolt Sámi Museum, Neiden, and at SALT in Oslo (2017–2018).

Documents on Contemporary Crafts, No. 5
Material Perceptions

Editors: Knut Astrup Bull and André Gali
Contributors: Glenn Adamson, Sarah R. Gilbert, Søren Kjørup,
Anders Ljungberg, Martina Margetts, Hilde Methi

Translation, proofreading, copyediting: Arlyne Moi
Translation of Anders Ljungberg's essay from Swedish: Megan Case
Art works © the artists/BONO
All texts © Norwegian Crafts and the authors

Parts of the article *Paying Attention to Material Responses in Local Ecologies* are
published in Britt Kramvig and Hilde Methi, 'Stories of Hope? A Journey in the
Dark European Arctic', in *Co-creating Tourism Research: Towards Collaborative
Ways of Knowing*, eds. Rene van der Dun, Carina Ren and Gunnar T. Johannesson
(London: Routledge, 2017).

Thanks to: Jorunn Veiteberg for helpful comments during the development of
the theme for this book, and special thanks to Art Council Norway for substantial
funding for the research and development of André Gali's text in this book.

Publication designed by: Aslak Gurholt (Yokoland)
Typeset in Tiempos Text 8.5/12.5
Printed on Munken Pure 120g, Arctic Paper, Sweden
Printed by: Livonia Print, Latvia

ISBN 978-3-89790-521-4
Publication funded by: Arts Council Norway

Bibliographic information published by the Deutsche Nationalbibliothek
The Deutsche Nationalbibliothek lists this publication in the Deutsche
Nationalbibliografie; detailed bibliographic data are available on the Internet at
www.dnb.de.

Norwegian Crafts
Rådhusgaten 20, 0151 Oslo, Norway
Phone: +47 97 07 87 31
Email: post@norwegiancrafts.no
www.norwegiancrafts.no

Arnoldsche Art Publishers
Olgastraße 137, D-70180 Stuttgart
Phone: +49 (0)711 64 56 18-0
Fax: +49 (0)711 64 56 18-79
Email: art@arnoldsche.com
www.arnoldsche.com